Children's Rights
and the Wheel of Life

The wheel of life is a mandala signifying the wholeness of the self, and the wholeness of a life. As drawn here it symbolizes that wholeness by representing the different stages of life from birth to death for the human being on the planet. The continuity of work from childhood through old age is expressed in the figures at work in different geographic settings around the world in the inner circle. Human rights, laws, and governments are depicted in the outer circle in assemblages from tribal council to western jury, and in the four symbols of the ringing bell, the ballot box, the scroll of laws, and the UN symbol. The mandala has been designed to evoke a sense of passage from stage to stage in all cultural-geographic regions of the world, and is meant to depict Everywoman and Everyman. It has been drawn especially for this book by the artist Helen Barchilon Redman.

Children's Rights
and the Wheel of Life

Elise Boulding

Transaction Books
New Brunswick, New Jersey

Library of Congress Catalog Number: 78-62890
ISBN: 0-87855-295-2 (cloth)
Printed in the United States of America

Library of Congress Cataloging in Publication Data

Boulding, Elise.
    Children's Rights and the Wheel of Life.

    Includes bibliographical references and index.
    1. Children's rights.   2. Social status.
3. Age groups.   4. Age discrimination. I. Title.
HQ796.B6848   301.43'14   78-62890
ISBN 0-87855-295-2

To Russell, Mark, Christine, Philip and William

Table of Contents

List of Tables

ix

FIGURES

Introduction and Acknowledgments

My sense of the autonomy, will and purposefulness of the very young stems from my own earliest memories of my own separateness, my own path, before I could read or write, and long before I was "allowed out on my own" in our neighborhood by strict but loving parents. My sense of the relatedness of the very young and the very old comes from my own mother's love of the elderly, and my frequent visits with her to the local home for the aged. There I saw, with my own eyes, people who were as individual and real as I, who like me could not go where they wanted to on their own.

Our own five children and their friends, and now our four grand-children, and the children I have taught, and been taught by, in Quaker Sunday Schools for twenty-five years and more, have all continually reenforced for me over the years my convictions about the active inner life, the social insight and the environment-shaping competence of the very young. The consistent underestimation of the understanding and abilities of the young on the part of adults around me has always enraged me, and continues to do so today. When it became clear that the International Year of the Child was going to continue this benevolent mater-nalist underestimation of childen, by dealing with protection from harm alone and leaving no room for enhancing the participation opportunities of children, I knew that I had to write this book and try to uncover the realities about what children can and do contribute to the social order. The initial opportunity came when Saul Mendlowitz, Director of the Institute for World Order's World Order Models Project asked me to prepare a background paper for that project on children's rights and world order. In preparing that paper, I felt the need to call attention to the fact that while the Year of the Child is focusing on those under four-teen, the fourteen to twenty year olds suffer from many of the constraints and disabilities of those much younger than they. As I studied the UN Declaration of Human Rights and the Declaration of the Rights of the Child, I became more and more aware of ageism as a phenomenon that excluded both the young and the old from participation in society according to their abilities, and established them instead as a vast protectorate inside the social order.

How to document the reality of that protectorate? Since I had already worked for ten years on United Nations data on the status of women, it was natural to turn to UN data to document the status of children and the elderly. That United Nations data has been supplemented in every way possible by reports of national and international bodies. I began with children as actors, shapers, contributors to society, and when I placed information on the constraints put on children side by side with information on their autonomous activities, there were times when I could hardly contain my rage. But along with rage was awe, reverence and love. The same experience was repeated when looking at the situation of the elderly. How to bring the two ends of the age spectrum to their rightful place in society? The concept of the wheel of life came as a great opening to me, a way of communicating to middle-years folks the oneness of life as we all move from decade to decade along our own individual life spans. By touching base inwardly with our own earliest years and, in anticipation, with our last years, a social empathy might be released in middle-years persons. Even more than empathy, a social wisdom could develop drawing on the perceptions of each age cohort. This wisdom could help break down ageism as those cohorts move through their own unique experience of life on the planet and bring their knowledge to bear on problems of human survival.

There are many complex legal and ethical issues regarding rights and protection which I have necessarily touched on in this book but have not been able to do justice to because of my own ignorance in these fields. I have not been concerned to come up with formulas for dealing with the young and the old, but with new ways of thinking about and relating to them. If the materials presented here help readers to get a new view of personhood at the extremes of the lifespan, I will be content. New policies to embody such perceptions will take time to formulate, but the process must begin now.

I have already mentioned my indebtedness to Saul Mendlowitz and the Institute for World Order in getting me started on this project. In addition, I have benefited very much from comments on the manuscript by various persons working with childhood and youth programs in voluntary associations, government agencies and the United Nations. In particular I would like to thank John Fobes, currently retiring Deputy Director General of UNESCO, Edward B. Marks, Associate Director of the International Year of the Child for the United Nations, Gloria Scott of the World Bank, and Irene Pinkau, Office Director of the International

Secretariat for Volunteer Services. I also wish to thank Celia Sudia, Luke Lee, Leslie J. Scallett, and Anne Cheatham, all of whom link a high level of professional expertise with strong civic concern and in various ways bring these concerns into government. I am grateful to Irving Louis Horowitz for his advice, encouragement, and willingness to publish the book. Most of all I am grateful to the children and young people with whom I have discussed the issues dealt with in this book for many years.

Needless to say, I bear full responsibility for the use I have made of all comments, for the interpretation of data presented, and for the views expressed on human rights and ageism.

Assembling the data used in this book was a complex task, and I wish to thank my research associates who assisted in this. Anita Cochran did the library search for international studies on children and youth; Dorothy Carson compiled the information on the children, youth and senior citizens-related NGOs; Scott Gassler extracted information from the *Human Rights Yearbooks* for 1970 and 1971; Janice Steinberg provided a review of some child development research; and Michael Greenstein and Herb Covey assisted with data retrieval from United Nations Yearbooks. Dorothy Carson and Alanna Preussner checked innumerable references, and Judy Fukuhara patiently and skillfully typed several versions of the manuscript.

It has been a particular delight to work once again with Helen Barchilon Redman, whose art work made the *Underside of History: A View of Women Through Time,* come alive as a book. I laid before her the wheel of life concept, and together we worked through details of conceptualization which resulted in the drawing which serves as frontispiece of this book. In my view, her wheel summarizes the entire message of the book.

Finally, I would like to thank Kenneth Boulding, my lifelong partner in exploring the worlds of youth and age, for his patience with my long periods of preoccupation while writing this book. There is much with which he will disagree here, but we share a deep love for the human family that overrides differences in interpretation of how that family should conduct its affairs on our planet.

Elise Boulding
Boulder Colorado
July 17, 1978

Human Time Tracks

The longing for wholeness is one of the most characteristic longings of our time. In the West that longing is sometimes expressed as a desire for "instant wholeness" — wholeness of the self with the universe. That kind of wholeness conveniently bypasses the complexity of incremental living, the inconvenience of having to be born, grow up, grow old and die in a social environment peopled with individuals all occupied with all inching along on their own time track. In most of the world, through most of history, there has been a keen awareness of that inching along process and mutual celebration of one another's passage from stage to stage on the wheel of life. Each person is reminded of what life has been by the presence of the young, and of what life will be by the presence of the old. Storytellers and prophets stretch the time sense into the past and the future.

In industrial societies people may move through life in touch with only their own group and their own present, never sensing the larger rhythm of their own life cycle and the cycles of birth, aging and death of families, communities and societies within which their own moment stands. These momentbound tenders of modernized societies are for the most part all in the second quarter century of their lifespan. Cut off by social design from interaction with young and old, they carry a heavy burden, including the burden of "protecting" the cohorts above and below them on the age ladder.

Both the narrowing of the time horizons and the heightened sense of human responsibility are consequenses of the many complex strands woven together in the experience of industrialization. On the one hand industrialization has meant discovery and further extension of human capacity through the inventions of the human mind. On the other hand it has meant a proliferation of institutional structures to handle those inventions, and to handle the population explosion they made possible. The human rights movement has emerged from the growing sense of contradictions between the poverty and suffering of the masses and the ac-

1

companying signals about unlimited human potential. That emergence has been a slow one.

The social vision, associated with the French revolution, which produced the Declaration of the Rights of Man in 1780, identified a part of humanity as human beings worthy to be rescued from oppression and assigned publicly recognized rights and opportunities, but only a part. In that declaration, slaves, various ethnic and religious groups, the poor, women, children, the old, prisoners and the mentally ill were all treated as residual categories of persons without full human rights. In the ensuing two centuries, social thought struggled with expanding concepts of personhood and rights of individuals. At the same time, the effects of westernization bore down so heavily on the young and the old, both in the West and elsewhere, that the doctrine of the helplessness of youth and age developed in just those circles most concerned with the rights of individuals. The convenience of age-segregated social patterns, initially evolved in the West to further the education of the young,[1] ensured that contradicting information from human development research about substantial unused human capacity and ability in the earliest and latest years of life did not penetrate to policy-making circles. What began as a humanitarian concern for the weak has resulted in a depersonalizing and devaluing of individual capacity in the young and the old through a doctrine of protection that has converted persons in these categories from subjects to objects of social concern.

The Universal Declaration of Human Rights adopted by the United Nations General Assembly in 1948 reflects the attitude that there are categories of persons needing rights of "protection,"but not requiring "rights of choice."[2] This declaration laid down that the rights and freedoms there enunciated applied to everyone "without distinction of any kind, such as race, colour, sex, language, religion, political or other opinion, national or social origin, property, birth or other status"(Article 2). Age, health and criminal status are not mentioned as classificatory principles, so presumably children, the old, prisoners and the mentally ill are not covered by the Declaration. If they are to be considered of "other status" covered by the Declaration, that has still to be spelled out. This book sets out to examine the case for adding age as a classificatory principle in the Declaration of Human Rights.

There is disagreement about whether human rights are legally or only morally binding upon states. According to one line of argument, human rights as enunciated in declarations and proclamations only become legally binding when they have been ratified as conventions by individual states. Waldock and Lee take the position that in general, subject to certain conditions, human rights are "rights which attach to all human beings equally, whatever their nationality" (Waldock 1965). "As such, the legal validity of their application cannot be rooted solely in a mere piece of paper signed and ratified by states. . . Rather, the analysis of the binding force of human rights must be approached also from their non-treaty sources: natural law, customary international law and general principles of law as recognized by civilized nations" (Lee 1972:311).

Whether human rights are seen as legally or only morally binding, statements about human rights in fact become criteria by which legal provisions for human well-being enunciated by individual nation states can be judged. No country in the world embodies in its laws the range of rights established in principle by the United Nations Declaration. The Declaration represents the aspirations of the world community for a baseline of freedom, justice and welfare of human beings. Legal enactment, country by country, may not be necessary in theory, but in fact such enactments help to make these rights operational for individual persons. Because such declarations represent a consensus on aspirations, they at the very least have the force of public opinion. When the values embodied in a human rights declaration fall short by more universalistic criteria, it becomes very important to work for the correction of such shortfalls, since persons affected by the shortfall are unlikely to be the beneficiaries of legal redress. What is being said in this study is that the failure to include the category of age in the UN Declaration represents such a shortfall, and should be corrected.

Considering children alone, eighteen of the thirty Articles in the Declaration of Human Rights do *not* apply to children.[3] Article 25 declares that children shall be protected, but does not refer to rights beyond the right of protection. Section 3 of Article 26 specifically denies children the right to choose their type of education, assigning this as a prior right to parents. The other fifteen Articles are of such general nature (for example, the right to peace) that they can hardly *not* apply to children, if only incidentally. The Declaration of the Rights of the Child consists of ten principles, only three of which assign rights to the child,[4] and the other seven assign protection and constraint "for the best interests of the child."

Lack of human rights protection of the elderly is more a matter of omission than commission; there is no special "Declaration of the rights of the elderly," for good or ill.

Can a case be made that consideration of the rights of children and the elderly should be included in the general process of consciousness raising about the human condition which is what the human rights movement is all about, or do the particular biological characteristics of these two populations make it appropriate to handle them primarily in terms of protection rights, placing them under the care of middle-years adults?

The concept of equal protection for all citizens does indeed require the making of distinctions that ensure equality in protection for persons in various life conditions. As has been well stated in a study of the constitutional rights of children in the United States:

> . . . a demand for equal protection cannot be a demand that laws apply universally to all persons. All laws classify, make distinctions. The legislature if it is to act at all must impose burdens upon or grant benefits to groups or classes of individuals. The demand for equality confronts the right to classify. "It is of the essence of classification that upon the class are cast . . . burdens different from those resting upon the general public . . . Indeed, the very idea of classificatioń is that of inequality . . . " [*Atchison, T & S.F.R.* v. *Matthews,* 1974 U.S. 96,106 (1899)]. Resolution of this dilemma is the doctrine of reasonable classification. The Constitution does not require that things different in fact be treated in law as though they were the same, only that those who are similarly situated be similarly treated. What is therefore barred are "arbitrary" classifications or discriminations" (Killian 1978:39,40).

It can indeed be argued that removal of age as a classificatory device for offering protection to the young and to the old would create a "child-blind" and an "elderly-blind" society that would deny the unique characteristics of each and create further injustice. To say that each individual is entitled to be treated as a unique person before the law is to give the courts a power of arbitrary decision over the lives of individuals which destroys the very rule of law that has evolved over the centuries to protect the individual from "ad hoc" justice (Killian 1978:44, 45).

Nevertheless, the slow but steady growth internationally of the children's rights movement and the senior citizen's rights movement since the sixties, suggest that current approaches to human rights at both ends of the life span are inadequate and need to be rethought. Looking at the youthful side, we must note that the children's movement is really two movements: the children's movement proper, consisting largely of urban area young people between the ages of eight and fourteen and supporting adults, and the youth rights movement, including high school and college age young people. Although this grouping represents a large age span, it is still the case that youth are classed with and treated as children with respect to many rights. The senior citizens' rights movement contains many preretirement members and some teenagers and young adults, as well as retired persons. The middle-years apostles of rights for children and youth often write with the high passion characteristic of outraged friends of the oppressed. Because of the emotional tone of some of their literature, it can be easily (and unjustifiably) ignored by rational people of good will. It is harder to ignore the elderly. There are fewer of them, they are *our* elders, and we ourselves will reach their status one day.

Ageism is a new word in the human rights vocabulary. UNESCO documents about youth sometimes use the term "anti-youth racialism," to refer to the hostility toward youth which is expressed both in public policy and private utterance, particularly in western countries. "Ageism" is a better term because it covers both ends of the age spectrum. Hostility toward the elderly receives more guarded expression, but we will see that it is there. Ageism is the denial of certain rights and responsibilities to persons simply because of their chronological age.[5]

Rights and responsibilities are twin aspects of the human rights concept, and neither has meaning without the other. Let it be understood whenever the term "rights" is used, that it means "rights and responsibilities."

Emphasizing the "responsibility" component of the word *rights* helps us to see how inappropriate a concept of rights is that only offers protection. Even the most democratic society has strong authoritarian elements, particularly when it is wearing its protective face. The individual to be protected has no option but to receive that protection when and how the protecting institutions of a society decree. As the UNESCO Report on Rights and Responsibilities of Youth (United Nations 1972b) says,

> Seen in this light, the responsibilities of young people, instead of meaning an opportunity for the young to take the initiative in actions which concern them and which ultimately concern society as a whole, seem more like duties imposed on them by adult society — the duty of submission to the authority of the family, the community or the State; the duty to receive education devised in the main by adults — or not to receive it if they belong to underprivileged social groups; the duty to work, often at an early age and under harsh conditions — or, conversely, to be the first to be affected by unemployment; the duty, lastly, to respect a world order established independently of them and which is becoming more and more alien to them (United Nations 1972b).

The duties of the elderly are not to be troublesome to their middle-years offspring, to do odd jobs and baby sitting when wanted, to give up (in the West at least) their jobs and community positions and control of their financial affairs, and be discreetly, dignifiedly invisible until they die.

Striking at the roots of ageism strikes at the root pathology of human relationship in all but the simplest, most egalitarian human societies: the drive to dominate, to mold the other. Authority, power, status, words we could not do without in describing modern social organization, turn sour under examination when we consider parent-child relations, or adult-elderly relations. Authority is the power of the middle-years folk to get children and the elderly to do what they want them to do without using force. The alternative intergenerational relationship of mutual respect and mutual support for continued growth throughout life is all too rarely seen. According to the American critic Farson, the vast literature on child development and child rearing has only assisted adults in replacing ignorant domination of the child by sophisticated domination (1974:3). The elderly will not have escaped either. Nor is that domination necessarily so subtle. Most western adults would not dare talk to their peers the way they talk to children or to their elderly parents. Nor would they themselves accept the interruptions, corrections, demands for attentiveness and instant displays of affection that children accept as a matter of course.

Mendel proposes the development of class consciousness on the part of children, and the waging of a class struggle between children and adults, as a way of getting children on a more equal footing with their protectors:

> Either recognition will be given to union rights and political rights of the childhood-adolescence social class — rights that will enable it within the class, to work out common attitudes on the basis of the positions of childhood-adolescence, and to claim effective powers, while preserving its own unique characteristics; or else the members of the rising generations, refused integration into the social order, not so much children as individuals reduced to infantile status, lacking in self-confidence, lacking confidence in adult society, may well be tempted to plunge into the depths of despair and rejection. Drug-taking, delinquency and neurosis are the escape routes when a person feels that he no longer holds his destiny in his hands and that all political paths are closed to him (Mendel 1972:8).

This is an unusual class war that he proposes, however, for it is one which is to release the positive, creative force of childhood in all of us. Adults, finally seeing children in their own personhood, will recognize and respect the inward state of being a child as a valuable and permanent part of the human personality, not something to be outgrown or overcome, and rediscover the child in themselves. It is a war which everyone will win. If the elderly also entered such a class struggle on behalf of their own personhood, then children and middle-years adults could learn to recognize the wise elder in themselves and to cherish it there and in the seniors among them. It is surely a richer conception of human individuality which considers the three stages of being, childhood, middle years and old age, as not simply succeeding one another but coexisting from birth, gradually and concurrently unfolding throughout life.

The theme of all human rights convenants, and the motif of all liberation movements, is participation in the shaping of one's own life and that of the society around one, and reasonable access to resources that will make that participation possible. In the case of children, either it is true that they are ignorant and incapable of significant social participation, and must be segregated from the adult world until they are twenty-one via the mechanism of the family to prevent social harm, or they are evolving participatory capabilities from early childhood and should be brought into decision-making involvement in the family and public spheres as their interests and abilities determine. If the latter is true, some substantial changes in the current United Nations Declaration of the Rights of the Child, and in associated concepts of the rights and responsibilities of children in families and communities will be required, both in custom and in law. More than that, some substantial changes in our conception of social process and the civic order will also be required. Since children represent well over fifty percent of the world's population at present, and are completely excluded from the reporting, evaluating and policy making processes of every society, an opening up of these processes to all young persons able to express interest and concern, of whatever age, would in the long run represent a revolution of unimaginable proportions in every country in the world, to say nothing of in the United Nations itself.

To speak of the revolutionary potential of more active civic participation by senior citizens will sound like nonsense to many. A not unfamiliar experience today is that older persons cling to power too long, and when they have been successfully shunted to purely honorary positions they take up a lot of time with excessively long speeches. Yet the age-grading practices that keep middle-years and older people from knowing and interacting with the new thinking and work of younger people, the lifelong habituation to dominance-submission relationships, and the general practice of removing older persons from specific operational participation where their experience and know-how might be relevant (this is what "retirement" really means), drives some senior citizens to these self-justificatory devices.

Trying to build a case for the participatory rights both of the young and the old across all the world's regions, ideologies and levels of industrialization between the covers of one book will not be an easy task. Yet the time for one-at-a-time liberation movements may be past. We are still in the throes of ethnic, racial and gender liberation movements. Until now, this is the way it had to be. But social attention spans are short; human energy is diffused over many social problems. Shall children be one more competing group in the fray, and next youth, and next the elderly? The concept of ageism can encompass all their problems, and move us further ahead than special group pleading.

The United Nations Year of the Child could be the occasion for a more basic rethinking of personhood and human rights because it points to the only minority human condition that is universally experienced, *childhood,* and the only human process that is universally experienced, *aging* . Here is an opportunity for every individual to link, in imagination, their own personal life spans with those of the young and old among us today, to reexperience and rethink the familiar old dominance patterns, and see afresh what they mean in terms of stunted physical, social and spiritual growth for everyone. This rethinking must be done in the context of great compassion for the middle-years adults — including myself, the author, and many of you, the readers — who unwittingly deny full personhood to the young and the old. Atlas-like, we carry the world quite unnecessarily on our backs. The heavy economic and social loading that present definitions of human rights place on middle-years adult roles will be explored later.

The same exercises of power that limit personhood, also support institutions and processes of social and economic injustice. Children, adults and elderly alike fall sick, go hungry, die prematurely from war, disease and hunger, because the microcosm of dominance-submission, center-periphery, haves/have-nots, is played out within and between nations as well as in families and local communities. The young and the old belong to the world's periphery. The centers of power will always let them be the first to go hungry, especially if they are poor; and most of the world's poor are either very young or very old. Welfare programs serve the young and old only of the middle and working classes, rarely the poor. The rhetoric of human rights must be exposed to the test of infant death rates and life expectancies of the poor in each society. In that test even some very wealthy nations fail badly.

The arena of public policy is both the first and the last place to look for significant social change toward a more just social order. If "UN Years" mean anything, they mean an opportunity to reexamine ends and means with regard to policy issues. The UN Year of the Child offers policymakers a fresh place to start with issues of human welfare: at the intersection of child, adult and local community relationships. A change in social attitudes toward children would affect every nook and cranny of society, and every person in it. Adult-child relationships offer a critical intervention point for breaking the vicious cycles of dominance behaviors that pervade public and international life. These patterns are laid down in the home with daily acts of inappropriate exercises of power, invisibly interwoven with the acts of human caring that sustain the institution of the family as a continuously viable setting for human growth. We may be unnecessarily sabotaging our present, and our children's future, by being blind to the inconsistencies and irrationalities of adult-child interaction in family and community in this century. Mass media programs about the right to a happy and secure childhood, and to a happy and secure retirement, cannot substitute for the actual experience of frank and honest confrontation between generations when perceptions, needs and interests differ, in a context of mutual acceptance of responsibility for each other. Neither can special feeding, health and education programs undertaken *for* children substitute for joint community projects carried out by adults and children together, in which capacities of the young to contribute to the welfare of all receives full recognition.

As a contribution to this local/global reexamination of intergenerational relations I offer the life cycle concept and a survey of the situation of the young and the old on the world scene in the context of that life cycle concept. Children will be considered first, and at greater length, since the Year of the Child is the focal event stimulating this study. A basic concept to keep in mind continually while reading this book however is that in the eyes of the law, and in the eyes of the societies that make the law, the young and the old are equally children.

First, the extent to which children and youth actually do participate in the economic, civic and social life outside and inside the family, in ways that can be explicitly identified as their own autonomous contributions, will be explored. This analysis will be largely based on United Nations data, supplemented by surveys from other international bodies and special studies when available. Instead of presenting data for all countries reporting to the United Nations, which would be difficult to digest, I have chosen fifteen countries representative of the major world regions for which to report data. Six countries are included from Euro-North

America, as contrasted with three each from Africa, Asia and Latin America. The emphasis on the West is partly because of the historical role of this part of the world in the last two centuries both in creating the problems of age and youth deprivation and in creating the rhetoric of human rights, and partly because more data is available from Europe than from anywhere else. For Africa, an ancient culture-region with fewer modern reporting facilities, there are inevitably more data gaps than for other regions.

The tables presenting this data are included in the text because I believe some readers will want to pore over them and tease out all the information which their minds and imaginations can muster. However, those who are not so interested in the numbers can skip the tables and simply follow the text, which interprets each table briefly. The purpose of the international comparisons is not to give in-depth analyses of different world regions, but to give some impressions of the similarities and differences in the situation of children in countries at various levels of industrialization, with different socio-economic and cultural patterns.

After examining the active, participatory roles of children and youth in their respective societies, we will look at children as objects of legal "protection," and explore the extent to which this protection helps or hinders the welfare of the young persons and the community. A restatement of the rights of children is offered.

Perhaps one of the most controversial aspects of this book is my lumping together of children, adolescents and youth under the rubric of "the child." Youth know better than middle-years adults how appropriate this is, since the restrictions placed on them stem from arbitrary conceptions concerning adulthood that leave them as constrained and helpless as those who are "really children." They will also know better than many adults how mature and responsible those who are "really children" often are.

Part III presents an overview of the life-cycle, birth-to-death rhythm for women and men. The situation of senior citizens will emerge from a comparative survey based on the same countries utilized in Parts I and II. The book closes with summary reflections on the life cycle perspective in human rights, and the importance of a partnership between persons in the first and third quarter centuries of life in creating the future social order.

NOTES

1. Age grading in folk societies does not have the same effect of segregation of knowledge because each youth group also carried out special tasks for the

whole village. Age grading thus represents a patterning of cooperation, not a patterning of segregation per se.

2. Hafen makes the following distinction between rights of protection and rights of choice: "Protection rights include the right not to be imprisoned without due process, rights to property, and rights to physical protection. No minimal intellectual or other capacity is necessary to justify a claim to those rights . . . 'Choice' rights, on the other hand, are the legal authority to make affirmative binding decisions of lasting consequence — marrying, contracting, exercising religious preferences, or seeking education" (Hafen 1977:1387).

3. These eighteen are: Articles 2, 6, 7, 10, 12, 13, 14, 16, 17, 18, 19, 20, 21, 22, 23, 26, 27, and 29. When there are several sections to an article, at least one section does not apply to children.

4. These three are: Principles 1, 3 and 4. See Appendix for the text of the United Nations Declaration of the Rights of the Child.

5. While ageism is a human rights concern expressed most frequently in the West, the underlying problems are found in all countries of the modern world. The statement of the problem, and the appropriate solution, will differ from country to country.

I.

Children and Youth as Subjects:
Thinkers and Doers

CHRONOLOGICAL AGE AND SOCIAL MATURITY

The legal ground for assigning *de jure* minority or "non-age" to children and youth is that they are physically, emotionally and socially immature beings who must be protected by adults until they reach full maturity and can cope on their own with society. In general, the term children is used for those under twelve or fourteen, and youth for those from the age of fourteen or fifteen to twenty-one or twenty-five, the age sometimes going as high as 30[1]. This means that society is protecting itself by legal means from having to incorporate young persons into full participation in society for what may be as long as half or more of the lifetime of those persons. Because age groups are designated in various ways in various societies, depending on custom, there is no standardized set of categories used in policy-making. Even within the same country, differing age barriers are set for different purposes. Utilizing the United Nations demographic reporting categories, I will use the following categories in this paper, corresponding roughly with social usage and reporting on children in many countries:

> 0-4, 5- 9—Children
> 10-14—Adolescents
> 15-19—Youth
> 20-24—Young Adults

The Year of the Child is focused on young persons up to their fourteenth year, in spite of some efforts to have the Year labelled for Children and Youth. Law and public policy, however, make minimal distinction between infants and twenty-year-olds. To underline the absurdity of this practice, and to call attention to the plight of the "infantalized" age group of fourteen to twenty year olds, all persons under twenty are included in the analyses that follow. Distinctions are made between infants, children and youth as necessary. If this sometimes causes confusion to the reader, let the reader think how much more confusion the "under twenty-one" social labelling causes to children and youth. The diversity of life situations of children and youth of various socio-economic groupings in countries of differing cultures, level of industrialization and political ideology cannot be over-emphasized. Not only will there be wide variation in the extent to which the most basic human needs of food and shelter are met and in the amount of labor force participation and availability of educational opportunities within and between countries, but there will be variation in the extent to which children and youth live in families, in institutions, in youth gangs or entirely on their own. No simple set of family and home images will suffice for picturing the settings in which the world's children and youth live out their first two decades of life. The attitudes of adults toward children vary as widely as the settings themselves.

Some societies treat all persons under twenty-five as legal minors; more common usage is to treat all under twenty-one as legal minors, with eighteen being established as the age of majority recently in a few countries. In many countries, a young person of twenty is as much a minor as a newborn babe. A United Nations study of *The Young Adult Offender* (1965:18) suggests that morphological, physiological, endocrinological and other aspects of physical development are not complete in many individuals until some time after age twenty-five, that psychological maturation peaks between twenty-five and twenty-nine years of age, and that social maturation is reached still later. While the studies cited may refer to some measurable body states, the significance of the concept of maturity in connection with adulthood and societal participation weakens when applied in this way. Erikson takes a totally different position in discussing the long childhood of "civilized" societies:

> Long childhood makes a technical and mental virtuoso out of man, but it also leaves a lifelong residue of emotional immaturity in him. While tribes and nations, in many intuitive ways, use child training to the end of gaining their particular form of mature human identity, their unique version of integrity, they are, and remain, beset by the irrational fears which stem from the very state of childhood which they exploited in their specific way (Erikson 1950:12).

The idea that there are built-in pathologies in modes of childrearing, particularly in the more "developed" and urban societies, which produce permanently immature and war-prone adults, is not a new one. It is gaining new ground through studies of partriarchy, militarism and the conquest syndrome by researchers working in the interdisciplinary fields of peace studies, future studies and human development. (Note, for example, Robertson 1976; Mendel 1971; and Boulding 1976a; 1978a).

Yet we pride ourselves in the West on having applied the findings of a century of child development research to the handling of infants, children and youth. We have structured their environments, designed their toys and learning materials, analyzed their readiness to receive teachings of various complexity. We are the potters, they are the clay. The friends of children in every age have always intuitively known that there was more to it than that. Now findings are creeping out of the child development laboratories that point to an autonomous self-organized learning process that begins with birth and can be easily interfered with by adults who treat the newborn as a blind and cuddly bit of protoplasm. (Stone, Smith and Murphy 1973). Observant workers with preschool children are noting the self-organizing nature of their learning, the complexity of judgments about body movements in time and space that they can develop when not over-organized in their activity, the sensitive mutual aid that goes on among them when they are left free to solve their own problems (Stallibrass 1974). Looked at with fresh eyes, many of the settings and activities we have programmed for the development of the young actually reduce their possibilities for developing their own particular capacities, based as these are on the body rhythms and perceptual functioning genetically unique to each individual.

The friends of children, the adults who watch and listen and learn from the younger members of the human race, are speaking up. Edith Cobb, in the book she spent a lifetime writing (*The Ecology of Imagination in Childhood* 1977) has noted the gifts of childhood to the human personality in the maintenance of plasticity of perception. In a moving synthesis of many recent discoveries about human development, she shows how children create the world anew through play. The discovery of the importance of that most spontaneous of all human activities to the continuous recreation of society, particularly as carried out by its younger members, is perhaps the major discovery of the twentieth century. Science cannot save us, but play may.[2]

The materials for a new and more respectful approach to children as learners, evaluators and shapers of social structure and social process have been rapidly accumulating since the days of Piaget's early work.

That the basic intellecting capacities are present very young, and that complex moral and political reasoning can take place by the age of twelve, has been established in the studies of cognitive, moral-emotional and political maturity by Piaget (1932), Susan Isaacs (1930), Kohlberg (1963), Erik Erickson (1964), Hess and Torney (1967), Elkind (1970), and others. Piaget identifies the ages of eleven and twelve as the period in which internal cognitive structures permit codification of rules by children, and the recognition that they are not immutable but can be changed by human decision. By the age of twelve a normally maturing individual is capable of all the formal operations of abstract thought required to make moral judgments in situations which are relevant to her. Piaget, working in the societal context of well-ordered Swiss society, sees the child as increasingly entering and accepting as her own the world of adult valuations. Kohlberg, working in the more anomic American scene, sees the child as effectively learning "what works" and using that knowledge hedonistically. An observer of twelve-year olds in a rural third world setting would find them hard at work beside older siblings and parents in the fields. It would be hard to tell them from adults, on the farm or in the city.

Kohlberg's research has led him to develop a six stage schema of development. Children begin to be able to function occasionally at level six, which means drawing on individual principles of conscience, by the age of ten. However, Kohlberg maintains that very few adults function fully at level six in their daily lives. Therefore "adulthood" is for the average person in fact an amalgam of lower levels of conformity and occasional eruptions of principle. His view that the majority of adults remain at a primitive level of moral reasoning, and that very few evolve toward altruistic moral judgments, is perhaps not unreasonable as we survey adult behavior around the world today. Children of the industrial world are segregated from adults at the very ages — ten to fourteen — when their cognitive capacities and social intuitions can and do produce, in their enclave settings, creative new social responses. This cuts short the further development of the children and prevents the adult world from receiving new perspectives. We know about the enclave creativity because there is a long history of experimental children's communities from the 1920s on. These arose in Europe in reaction to an earlier extreme authoritarianism in relation to children. There was Makarenko's Gorki colony in the Soviet Union in the 1920s, Homer Lane's Little Commonwealth in England, 1914-18, and A.S. Neill's communities in Germany and Austria before he started Summerhill in England. There were also in England Susan Isaacs, Olive Kendon, Teddy O'Neill, Alex Bloom and others less well recorded.[3] There were also young teenage groups in Germany that travelled to Palestine to found kibbutzim (Bettelheim 1969).

If we go back to the preindustrial era in Europe we can see a great deal of evidence that persons ten to twelve and over were functioning as adults in having to take full responsibility for themselves and contribute to the economic welfare of their own family and the economic productivity of the employment setting in which they were placed. The film, "Invention of the Adolescent," produced by the Canadian Broadcasting Corporation in 1970, documents the transition from preindustrial to postindustrial society for children of the first world, and shows how recent and contrived is our image of the adolescent as immature and irresponsible. The only vestige remaining of that earlier role is today's child actor, a carefully tended descendant of the robust companies of child actors of sixteenth century England and Europe (Shapiro 1977).

Research on the assignment of responsibility to children in nonindustrial societies, based on an examination of Human Relations Area Files materials on fifty cultures (Rogoff et al. 1976) indicates that there is a modal cultural assignment of social responsibility in the five to seven age range for sixteen of the twenty-seven activity and attribution categories examined. These include care of siblings, tending animals, household chores, gathering materials and running errands, responsibility for anti-social behavior, practical training through imitation, teaching of social consciousness, attribution of common sense to the child, considering child's character to be fixed, change in form of punishment from that used earlier, shift to peer-group focus for children, playing games by rules, same sex play groups, sex differentiation, inculcation of cultural traditions.[4] Between the ages of seven and nine children in many cultures are independent of the primary family unit and may, for example, be sent to live with mother's brother. By puberty, the modal situation in these fifty cultures is that the child "no longer lives in the family situation but establishes an independent family or lives in a communal situation with peers or same-sex groups." (Rogoff P:256). Some form of public test of maturity takes place, and adult clothing is adopted. There are still further steps to be taken before full civic status in tribal councils is achieved, but there is a general acceptance of the capacity of children and youth to contribute to the economic and social welfare of the community from the age of five on.

Maturity as used in the Western literature on human development is more a mystification than a clarification of the meaning of adulthood, and needs to be substantially redefined before it becomes a criterion for full participation in society. We will see in the following pages that even in our own century children from a very young age are required, as are women, to do heavy physical labor that in theory is not suited to their physical capacities. They serve and tend their own parents, and become parents themselves, all while still legally minors. They fight wars, mount relief operations, design international institutions — all between the ages of twelve (or younger) and twenty one. It is only necessary for each of us to remember back to our own childhood, what we coped with, what insights we gained, to realize how much children endure, how much they have to give that adults never notice (Milgram and Sciarral 1974; Boulding 1962 and 1967b), What is maturity?

CHILDREN AND YOUTH IN THE LABOR FORCE

The picture that will be painted in this section of the extent of participation of children in the labor force, and of the ambiguous responses to that reality by adults, needs to be set in a broader context of the meaning of work in modern society, and of the distribution of the fruits of labor throughout the social system. Children, like women, and the elderly, are most valued in settings where there is high labor-intensity.The more industrialized a society becomes, the more children are given the most menial and repetitive tasks. It is "useful" to have them remain marginal. The increased wealth of the technological society does not however go to the poorest workers, whether children, women or men, but rises like cream to the top and feeds those who are already well fed. The structures of distribution, like the structures of civic participation, operate to exclude the poor. The general theme of this book is that there is a need to acknowledge what children and the elderly do, and enable them to do it under conditions of greater dignity and autonomy. However, it makes little sense to call for recognition and autonomy in a society structured to create wealth by exploitation, and then to divert that wealth from those who need it most.

My own analytic skills lie in uncovering the inventive and adaptive skills of human beings, and showing how they use the ingredients in hand for making livable microspaces inside social structures that constrain their humanness. But the problems of inequitable social structures must also be addressed. I ask the reader to bear in mind that far more has to be done to create a more humane society than deal with the problems of ageism described in this book. On the other hand as John Muir has said, any one thing you pick up is connected to the whole universe. In dealing with ageism, no other aspect of human life as lived in society can remain untouched. In particular, the gap created in capitalist society between the conditions of production and the enjoyment of its fruits must be dealt with. So must the gap between North and South created in the colonial

era. Unless there is a new International Economic Order no human beings of any age can have true wellbeing, for rich and poor alike will be
psychically crippled.

At present, adults professionally concerned with children are
sometimes confused about what position they should take in regard to
child labor. The anti-child-labor movement in Europe and North
America was very strong from the late nineteenth century through the
early decades of this century. Factory conditions and working hours had
deteriorated from an earlier standard set when families worked in factories as household groups, and were usually terrible for young bodies
and minds. Much of the spirit of protection that we see in the 1970s stems
from the necessary drive to protect children from these abuses of an
earlier era of the industrial revolution. Todays's generation of middle-
class children in the urban areas of both the more and less industrialized
countries are told to run and play, or to study more. The children of the
poor comb the streets for odd jobs or adventure. Most of these children
feel trapped, whether in the streets, in the playroom or in the
schoolroom, and would love to have their own job. Their despair is
variously exhibited in high frequencies of suicide, or drug and alcohol
use, and in rising school dropout rates. These are not only western
phenomena. In Japan, suicides by children between the ages of five and
fourteen rose from forty-six in 1965 to ninety in 1975 and were expected
to go considerably higher in 1977 (Murata 1977). School dropout rates in
developing countries go as high as two-thirds of the children enrolled in
primary school (United Nations 1977b/1). Why this despair? Play is an
empty word in the absence of free spaces where a child can shape her environment to suit her needs and desires. A recent UNESCO study of urban children in cities around the world brings this out with startling clari-
ty (Lynch 1977). The despair affects both the younger, ten to fourteen
year group and the older, fifteen to nineteen age group, particularly
where unemployment is high.

The situation is different in the countryside. In the world's rural areas
most children are at work by ten or twelve years of age. In fact, they are
frequently at work from the age of five. Boys work in the fields, girls
help with younger children, or help in household and field work also.
They have always done so, from the earliest times. With urbanization,
working conditions become harder — whether we are talking about ancient or modern urbanization. In the era of the 1970s, when a high social
value is set on keeping children in school, there is little incentive to report
child labor, and most children work[5] unrecorded, whether for their own
parents or as wage laborers. The fact that Table 1 records some under-
fifteen labor should be taken as indicating the tip of the iceberg. There

Table 1. Economically Active Children and Young Adults, by Sex

	Africa			Asia		
	Egypt	Algeria	Tanzania	Japan	Philip-pines	Thailand
% Economically Active Population under 15						
All	3.8	1.3	6.5	--	4.7	10.9
Males	6.2	2.0	6.5	--	5.7	10.1
Females	1.3	0.6	6.6	--	3.6	11.7
% Economically Active Population 15-19						
All	34.1	34.7	62.5	36.1	41.3	77.3
Males	58.6	65.7	59.3	36.5	52.4	77.4
Females	7.3	3.7	65.5	35.7	31.5	77.2
% Economically Active Population 20-24						
All	43.5	44.0	77.6	77.2	53.8	84.0
Males	83.7	93.4	84.1	83.5	76.0	89.2
Females	7.8	3.6	73.1	70.8	34.4	79.0

SOURCE: Table 1, "Total and Economically Active Population by Sex and Age Group," (United Nations, 1975f).

are many child workers beneath the surface. The lower age limit is not specified in the reporting, but it is usually age ten.

Table 1 organizes information about economically active children and young adults for four world regions: Africa, Asia, Latin America and Euro-North America. The specific countries representing each region were chosen partly to represent the range of cultures in each region, and partly because they reported information on children in the labor force to the United Nations Statistical Office. Many countries do not report this information to the United Nations. Africa, Asia and Latin America all have large rural subsistence sectors with the exception of Japan, so many of the employed children are in fact employed as rural wage laborers.

There are substantial differences from country to country in the percent of under-fifteens reported in the labor force, both within and between regions. We see for example that Africa, and Asian countries, have from one to eleven percent of under-fifteens reported in the labor force, as contrasted with under three percent for Latin America. In Euro-North America only Hungary, Spain and the United States report under-fifteens employed, with Spain having the high for Europe of 1.7 percent. In general, we expect more boys than girls under fifteen to be reported in the labor force, since there is a very widespread cross-cultural image of women and girls as homebound. Yet this expected tendency is counteracted by Tanzania, Thailand and Hungary, all of which report

Table 1 (cont'd)

	Euro-North America					Latin America		
France	Hungary	Sweden	Spain	United Kingdom	United States	Colombia	Mexico	Peru
--	0.6	--	1.7	--	0.6	2.8	1.5	1.4
--	0.3	--	2.2	--	0.9	4.3	2.2	1.6
--	0.9	--	1.1	--	0.4	1.2	0.9	1.3
37.1	47.4	31.1	51.5	58.3	34.8	42.9	35.2	28.9
42.8	45.8	32.9	65.9	60.8	40.3	66.3	49.9	39.8
31.3	49.1	29.3	36.7	55.7	29.2	21.8	20.9	17.7
72.7	79.0	57.7	60.5	75.1	68.0	56.3	50.6	52.8
82.6	91.5	62.0	81.0	89.9	80.9	89.8	79.6	80.2
62.3	66.2	53.3	39.6	60.1	56.1	26.3	24.1	25.8

more female than male employment under fifteen. By the time these young people reach age fifteen, they are much more strongly represented in the labor force, on every continent. In Tanzania, Thailand, Hungary, Spain, and the United Kingdom, fifteen to nineteens are close to or more than half the labor force. Considered by gender, more than half the males are in the labor force in most countries. Females are from one-fifth to two-thirds in the labor force except in strongly Moslem countries like Egypt and Algeria. In the twenty to twenty-four age group there appears to be close to the maximum labor force participation by gender that a country will be experiencing. In short, in terms of economic responsibility as revealed in the public data of a country, adolescents as well as youth are clearly a part of the recognized labor force, though in smaller numbers, in every region. If we look for the highs in under-fifteen labor force participation in countries not shown in the table, we find that in Africa, Gabon has 16.9 percent adolescents in the labor force; in the Americas, Haiti has 24.2; in Asia, Nepal has 14 percent; in Europe, both the Netherlands and Portugal have 4.5 percent. These are not insignificant figures for adolescents in the public, officially enumerated labor force.

Are there any particular patterns of socio-economic conditions for a country that are conducive to large scale employment of younger persons? To answer this question, we have brought together in Table 2 data on growth rates of the population as a whole, the urban population and the Gross National Product, as well as figures on the percent of the population that is rural and the GNP per capita, for the countries of Table 1.[6] Comparing the two tables, it is interesting to note that Tanzania, which had the second largest proportion of under-fifteens to nineteens employed in the entire panel of countries, also has the largest rural population and, the most rapid urbanization. Its economic growth rate is moderate — neither high nor low. Recording of the participation of the young in the labor force may be associated with the social and economic egalitarianism characteristic of that country. Thailand which records the most under-fifteens in the labor force of any country is like Tanzania predominantly rural. Its economic growth is also intermediate, between the high of Japan and the more modest rate of the Philippines. In Latin America, the pattern is reversed. The most under-fifteens in the labor force, in Colombia, is associated with a more urban society with a relatively high economic growth rate. In Europe, a high economic growth rate is associated with having the most under-fifteens in the labor force, in Spain. From the data available to us, we must provisionally conclude that no particular socio-economic patterns are associated with greater incidence of child labor. Rather, under-fifteen participation in the labor force can be associated with a variety of economic and social conditions. Egypt, Tanzania, the Phillippines, Thailand, Spain and Colombia are very different kinds of societies in terms of culture, economic system, level of industrialization and political ideology. They all have

Table 2. Economic and Social Variables
Affecting the Status of Children and Youth

	Africa			Asia		
	Egypt	Algeria	Tanzania	Japan	Philippines	Thailand
Population Growth Rate, 1965-1973[a]	2.5	3.4	2.8	1.2	3.0	3.0
Urban Growth Rate[b]	7.5	33.3	32.8[d]	--	--	--
% Rural Population[c]	52.0	73.5	94.9	24.3	36.8	91.2
GNP[a]	250	570	130	3,630	280	270
Economic Growth Rate, 1965-1973[a]	0.8	4.3	2.6	9.6	2.6	4.5

[a] Boulding Global Data Bank, n.d.

[b] Table 6, "Urban and Total Population by Sex, 1966-1974 (United Nations, 1975e).

[c] Boulding, Carson, Nuss and Greenstein (1976).

two percent or more of their under-fifteens in the enumerated labor force.

Generalizations about socio-economic determinants of child labor force participation cannot really be made on the basis of this brief analysis, since work has different meanings and characteristics in societies with different economic and political systems and different levels of productivity.

A recent study of the economic activities of children in a village in Bangladesh (Cain, 1977:201-228) throws a little light on the type of labor by age and sex behind the figures for third world countries in Table 1. Based on careful observations and time-budget study, Cain finds that children begin work at the age of four, and that boys by the age twelve (or somewhere between the ages of ten and thirteen) become "net producers." (That is, they produce more than is required simply to maintain themselves.) By age fifteen they have compensated for their own cumulative consumption and by age twenty-two for the cumulative consumption of one sister also. Girls are generally kept from field work, and as home tasks are more limited, are thus rated as less productive. (This evaluation may be questioned. When the data are further examined, it is found that girls do engage in all kinds of field work including care of animals and fishing, excepting only plowing, transplanting and cutting jute. They are found at work in nineteen categories out of twenty-five work catagories, although in lesser numbers than boys.)

Table 2 (cont'd)

	Euro-North America					Latin America		
France	Hungary	Sweden	Spain	United Kingdom	United States	Colombia	Mexico	Peru
0.8	0.3	0.7	1.7	0.4	1.0	2.8	3.5	2.9
--	10.4	--	--	-2.0^e	--	15.9	11.5	10.2
58.1	58.2	55.8	54.6	16.6	53.0	43.0	70.4	64.8
4,540	1,850	5,910	1,710	3,060	6,200	440	890	620
5.0	2.7	2.4	5.3	2.3	2.5	3.1	2.8	1.8

^{d}Urban Growth Rate, 1967-1973.

^{e}Urban Growth Rate, 1966-1973.

In terms of hours of work, children four to six average three hours; seven to nine, five hours; ten to twelve, seven hours and thirteen to fifteen, nine hours. There are slight differences in averages for male and female children but at some ages girls work longer hours, at other ages boys work longer hours. In general, from thirteen years and up children are working the same number of hours as adults. This is true for the poorest subsistence families as well as for the landed families. In the latter the number of working hours are shorter for both adults and children, but they put in the same working day. While findings from a Bangladesh village can hardly be generalized to all rural areas, they confirm frequent reports from rural areas in all parts of the world that children begin working at the age of four and do an adult's day's work by age twelve. This was certainly true in rural England at the beginning of the industrial revolution (Samuel 1975:266-267).

In the United States, with the most energy-intensive agriculture in the world, one out of every four agricultural workers is under sixteen, according to 1969 estimates. Employing children under twelve for farm labor was made illegal as recently as 1974. An investigation in 1975 found that children under twelve continue to work in substantial numbers with inadequate protection in regard to health and length of working hours (up to ten hours a day) in the states of Washington, Oregon and Maine (American Friends Service Comittee, 1976). Health data on child workers, both migrant and local family workers, suggests that the view that agricultural labor is healthy for children does not hold for child workers who suffer high rates of pneumonia and other respiratory diseases, or exposure to dangerous pesticides used to spray crops. Unfortunately, child labor stimulates extreme emotional responses. The emotional revulsion against the idea of having children working in the fields at all works against the establishment of sensible regulatory devices that would ensure children working reasonable hours under reasonable conditions.

There is an enormous difference between child labor in the countryside and child labor in the city. It is in the world's urban areas that under-fifteen workers are the most vulnerable, and have the least protection. In fact, young workers right up to the age of twenty-five lack the protections that workers over twenty-five may receive, according to a UNESCO report (United Nations 1976d). They bear the brunt of unemployment (sometimes as high as fifty percent unemployed) and they work much longer hours for lower wages. Legal limits suggest what the underlying realities might be. In Thailand and Singapore, children under fourteen are limited to a thirty-six hour week; most countries limit sixteen-year-olds to a thirty-six hour week, though in Japan they can work forty-two hours. In the Netherlands, young workers receive a percentage of the full adult wage for their work, according to the following age schedule (United Nations 1972b:40):

Age	%		Age	%
14	30		19	60
15	35		20	70
16	40		21	80
17	45		22	90
18	50			

While many unions do not stipulate an age limit on union membership, the practice is to exclude them from work councils until they are twenty-one or even twenty-three, thus effectively disenfranchising them.[7] A few unions defend the interests of their younger workers, particulary in socialist countries, but most apparently do not. Frequently the stipulated age for union membership is higher than the minimum age for admission to employment. There is considerable evidence that working conditions can be very punitive for children and youth, beyond what they are for older workers. Since youth are also better educated than their parents, and taught to have higher aspirations, the alienation of children and youth from the concept of work as a positive social value is often strong (United Nations 1976d).

Since the need for children and youth to work, both under-fifteens and the over-fifteens, appears to be overriding in societies at all stages of development, enfranchising them to negotiate their conditions of work side by side with older workers ought to be seriously considered. Antiwork laws do not provide a viable approach.

MILITARY SERVICE FOR YOUTH

If there has been confusion about policies regarding children and youth in labor force, there has never been any confusion about policies regarding military service of young persons. Minors have always been put into armies, and there have been many teen-age military heroes in history. One of the Prophet Mohammed's greatest generals was turned down for military service by Mohammed at the age of fourteen, but accepted at fifteen as an officer. Alexander the Great was a veteran of many battles by the time he was twenty. Henry V served as a general in his father's army, conducting the war against Wales, at the age of fourteen. Table 3A gives a picture of age, and length of service for those of the fifteen countries we are studying for which data was available. It will be seen that most of these countries had compulsory conscription in

1968, that the service ranged from one to three years, and that most of them did not have provision for alternative service for conscientious objectors. (None of these countries conscript young women.)[8] Young people who have been reared in dissenting pacifist sects such as are found in all major religious traditions of the world frequently suffer severe persecution, imprisonment and sometimes the death penalty when they are drafted into their country's military, because of the lack of provision for the pacifist conscience. Table 3B shows the age of entry into military service for all of the fifty-nine countries for which data was available, and it will be seen that most young people become liable for military service by age eighteen. It is not difficult to see that a substantial part of the burden of national defense in most countries rests on the shoulders of youth under twenty-one.

ADOLESCENT AND YOUTH AS BEARERS
AND REARERS OF CHILDREN

We are so accustomed to the legal and social rhetoric about protecting minors that we forget that a great deal of the work of rearing and protecting the young is done by persons who are themselves still minors.

Table 3A. Military Service Requirement
by Age and Length of Service, 1968

	Africa			Asia		
	Egypt	Algeria	Tanzania	Japan	Philip- pines	Thailand
Conscription	yes	--	--	no	yes	yes
Provision for COs	none	--	--	--	none	none
Call-Up Age	18	--	--	--	21	21
Period of Service	3 yr	--	--	--	3 yr	2 yr

[*]Conscription was discontinued in the United States in the 1970s.

SOURCE: Prasad and Smythe (1968).

Close to thirteen million of the sixty million women who became mothers in 1975 became parents before they became adults . . . Early childbearing is increasing everywhere, is emerging as a serious problem in many countries, and has reached alarming levels in others [where it is associated] with serious health, socioeconomic and demographic implications for young women, young men, their offspring, and indeed, for the whole society . . . Adolescent pregnancy is a serious threat to the life and health of young woman . . . whether the birth occurs in or out of marriage, findings by 160 delegates from thirty-nine countries at the First Interhemispheric Conference on Adolescent Fertility, Airlie House, Va., 1976. See *11 Million Teenagers* 1976:6).

The significant aspect of teenage pregnancy, as we can see from Table 4, is that it is not simply a phenomenon of less industrialized countries, but of the most industrialized countries, with the United States a leading producer of teenage childbearers. The "prime time" for women to bear children is considered to be between the ages of twenty to twenty-four. Earlier childbearing involves high risk to the mother, and considerably lowered chances of survival for the infant. Yet in many countries large numbers of teenage girls take these risks, at least in part because their minority status prevents them from gaining access to the preventive measures they could employ if they knew about them. In *no* society does minority status make sexual activity inaccessible, whatever the official norms might be.

Table 3A (cont'd)

	Euro-North America					Latin America		
France	Hungary	Sweden	Spain	United Kingdom	United States	Colombia	Mexico	Peru
yes	yes	yes	yes	none	yes*	yes	yes	yes
yes	none	yes	none	--	yes	none	none	none
20	18	18	21	--	18	18	18	19
16 mo	--	1 yr	16 mo– 2 yr	--	2 yr	2 yr	1 yr	2 yr

Table 3B. Age of Entry into Compulsory Military Service for Fifty-Nine Countries, 1968

	Age				
	17	18	19	20	21
Number of Countries	1	28	4	15	11

SOURCE: Prasad and Smythe (1968).

Table 4. Number of Births per 1,000 Females aged 15-19, Selected Countries

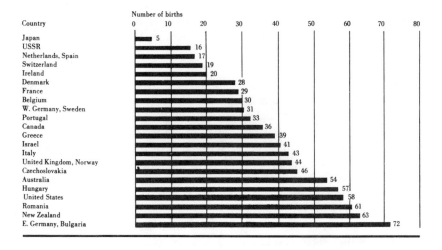

Source: 11 Million Teenagers (1976:7)

The onset of fertility ranges from age ten to the mid-teens.[9] One of the tragedies for girl children is that while the majority of them live in countries where family planning services are available and abortion is legal under certain conditions, the ten to fifteen year olds who are at risk of pregnancy almost never have access to these services. Even fifteen to nineteen-year-olds are drastically underserviced in comparison to older women. Teenage women can and do seek illegal abortion, in ignorance of safer methods, and a recent study in Cali, Columbia estimated that complications from illegal abortions were the leading cause of death of women aged fifteen to thirty-five (Eckholm and Newland 1977:16).

What is the life situation of these young childbearers? In Table 5 we see what proportion of the total population these under-fifteen and under-twenty young women are, how many children under five the over-fifteens have to look after (the child-woman ratio is the number of children under five per 1000 women fifteen to forty-nine), what the legal age of marriage for women is, and what the actual marriage rates are for under-fifteens and fifteen-to-nineteens. These figures, plus the number of births per women of the fifteen to nineteens (pre-fifteens are rarely reported) and the life expectancy of young persons at birth, will give us some idea of patterns of life for women under twenty. We may note first that in Africa, Asia (except for Japan) and Latin America, those under fifteen already represent close to fifty percent of the population, and those under twenty are closer to sixty percent of the total population. In Europe and North America the figure is more like one-quarter under fifteen, one-third under 20. Third world young women live in a "country of the young," and have high child-woman ratios. While the legal age of marriage varies from twelve to eighteen, with highs and lows found on all continents at all levels of development, few except in Latin America marry under fifteen.

Even by age twenty only from one-third to one-half of the young women in Table 5 are married, and the proportion of all live births to the under-twenties is not as high in the third world countries as in some first world countries, as has already been pointed out. Many of the third world women will have had stillbirths of which there is no record, and have already lived half or more of their expected life span. (If they have born children before the age of twenty, their life expectancy will be considerably shorter than the figure listed in the last line of the table.)

We have no way of knowing what the life situation by age twenty is of the one-half to two-thirds of young women not married. Some live at home and work for their parental family; some are living in consensual unions, long or short-term, some with other young women, some alone, and some in institutional settings such as the factory dormitories traditional for young women textile workers in Japan. Some will marry later, some will never marry. At any one time roughly one-third of all women over fifteen will be legally unpartnered. Young twelve-year-old brides probably do not have their own household, but live as helpers in the home of the husband's family.

The responsibilities of the teenage married woman who is also a mother may be light compared to the responsibilities of the teenage unmarried mother. Table 6 shows the out-of-wedlock births in the United States for the 1960s and 1970s. A majority of these young women keep their babies, and have their lives programmed for them in terms of the double task of working to support the mother-child household, and of being sole parent to the child.[10] Economic support from the father, even if paternal filiation is legally established, is rare. What percentage of these young mothers will eventually marry we do not know. We do know that they receive a disproportionately small share of publicly funded family services.

Married or unmarried, teenage mothers, like older mothers, bear the primary responsibility for parenting. Society neither expects parenting from fathers, of any age, nor gives them training for it. Among the most disadvantaged categories of minors then, are the unwed adolescent and teenage mothers, and their illegitimate offspring. While the United Nations Declaration of the Rights of the Child guarantees whatever rights

Table 5. Population Ratios, Marriage, Childbearing, and Life Expectancy for Children and Young Adults

	Africa			Asia		
	Egypt	Algeria	Tanzania	Japan	Philip-pines	Thailand
% Population Under 15 (-15)[a]	43.6	50.0	45.3	25.0	44.5	45.9
% Population Under 20 (-20)[a]	54.0	59.3	53.9	34.0	54.0	56.6
Child/Woman Ratio[b]	702	940	--	291	729	697
Legal Age of Marriage for Women[b]	16	--	--	16	14	--
Marriage Rates, - to 15[c]	--	d	--	d	0.8	--
Marriage Rates, 15 to 19[c]	48.6	52.3	--	34.5	36.9	--
Births Per Woman, 15 to 19[b]	.1921	.1276	--	.0122	.0772	.0831
Life Expectancy For Women[b]	53.8	50.7	40.5	74.3	53.4	58.7

[a]United Nations (1975e)

[b]Boulding, Nuss, Carson and Greenstein (1976).

[c]Table 12,"Marriages by Age of Bridegroom and Bride" (United Nations, 1975e).

there are, to all children regardless of birth (Principle 1), in fact only twenty-two countries recognize one status for all children whatever their circumstances of birth.[11] In all the rest, both the unwed mothers and their illegitimate children carry lifelong handicaps. Young mothers must go through legal procedures to establish paternal filiation in order even to be able to give a name to to a child. In some countries, it is required that the father's parentage be established in court if possible to do so; once paternal filiation is so established, the child must carry its father's name and nationality, and only the father has legally recognized authority over the child. This is true even though the mother may be the sole support and rearer of the child. Daily responsibility without recognized authority is one of the worst burdens young unmarried mothers have to bear. The legal supports for irresponsible fatherhood, and the legal constraints on responsible motherhood, are extremely injurious to everyone concerned, most of all the offspring. Even when the mother can establish both legal filiation and authority, the child may frequently not inherit from or be assisted by the mother's parental family. The cards are stack-

Table 5 (cont'd)

Europe and North America						Latin America		
France	Hungary	Sweden	Spain	United Kingdom	United States	Colombia	Mexico	Peru
24.8	22.4	21.2	29.1	25.5	28.7	47.9	47.2	44.4
33.7	31.8	28.2	37.3	32.8	38.1	57.6	57.5	55.0
298	332	303	382	336	488	779	726	735
15	14	18	12	16	18[e]	12	14	12
.008	.04	.007	[d]	--	.23	1.2	2.3	1.7
19.7	38.2	7.0	12.9	25.8	32.8	35.2	40.8	27.7
.0635	.1487	.0486	.0278	.1021	.2536	.1115	--	.1187
75.3	71.9	76.5	71.9	74.9	70.8	45.0	63.7	55.5

[d] Only marriage rates for - to 19 were reported.

[e] Varies from state to state.

ed against the unwed mother and the illegitimate child in every conceivable way. Tribal customs which provide formulas for the legitimacy of any child born regardless of circumstances of birth are disappearing, to be replaced by inhumane "modern" laws.[12] Given the rapid increase in percent of out-of-wedlock births in many countries, including the most industrialized, this creates a serious long-term problem as regards responsible citizenship in the world community. The full burden of this problem is placed squarely on the fragile shoulders of children and youth.

While the burdens placed on adolescent and teenage women are very heavy and may substantially shorten their life expectancy, it should also be emphasized that many of these unmarried child-mothers do in fact cope successfully with the burdens placed upon them. Many do make homes for their children, do work to support them, do provide nurture when they themselves have to do without nurture. They give responsibility to their own children very early, just as they have had to take responsibility very early. Most researchers study the "problem" teenage mothers. Few look at the ones who manage well.[13] The strengths such

**Table 6. Percent of Births to Females Aged 14-19
that were Out-of-Wedlock, by Single Years of Age,
United States, 1960-64 and 1970-74**

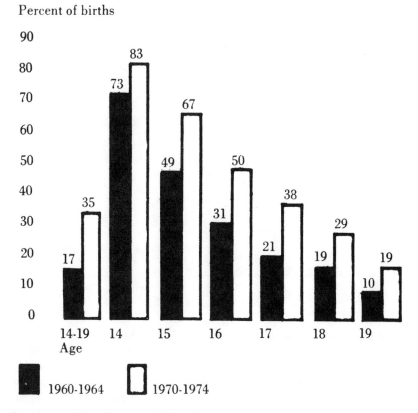

Percent of births

Source: *11 Million Teenagers* (1976:14).

young women exhibit under great and prolonged stress are an indication
of the resources available to society if they were allowed to participate in
its shaping on more equal terms.

NURTURANCE OF ADULTS AND PEER GROUP
BY CHILDREN AND YOUTH

The previous section has suggested the important role children must
inevitably play as partner to the mother who is herself scarcely out of
childhood in mother-headed households. The child as working partner in
the family is as old as the phenomenon of the family itself. The child as

nurturer of the younger and older members of the household is a role that is apt to be overlooked. On the other hand, uncounted numbers of small children in the third world (and the first) are cared for by siblings aged eight to twelve (Stein 1965:66). On the other hand, children also provide nurturance to their own parents and grandparents. While this phenomenon is present in all societies, it is most apt to be recorded in the West, where there is an ample supply of professionally trained workers making observations on family behavior. This child-to-adult nurturance comes poignantly to view in discussions of abusing parents in the United States. De Mause takes note of this phenomenon:

> Present day social workers who visit "battering" mothers are often astonished at how responsive little children are to the needs of their parents: "I remember watching an eighteen month old soothe her mother, who was in a high state of anxiety and tears. First she put down the bottle she was sucking. Then she moved about in such a way that she could approach, then touch, and eventually calm her mother down (something I had not been able to begin to do). When she sensed her mother was comfortable again, she walked across the floor, lay down, picked up her bottle, and started sucking it again" (De Mause 1974:20).

Another extraordinary observation by DeMause on the nurturing role of the small child:

> I have catalogued over five hundred paintings of mothers and children from every country, and found that the paintings showed the child looking at, smiling and caressing the mother at a date prior to the ones showing the mother looking at, smiling and caressing the child, rare actions for a mother in any painting (1974:20-21).

A recent exploration of the extent to which children and teenagers counsel and give emotional support to parents in times of stress, suggests that this is a very widespread phenomenon (Boulding 1978b). Historically, children have acted as servants to their parents, at least in the West, and in preindustrial Europe this was well worked out in terms of exchange of children between households, so each set of parents trained their neighbor's children in household skills (Boulding 1976a). A number of etiquette books were written for children in the late Middle Ages and Renaissance advising them on their servant role. It is clear that children had to be very resourceful, from the kind of situations set out as teaching examples in these books (Furnival 1930;1931). One of the least noticed times when children nurture parents is during a death in the family.[14] The nurturing role of the child is even more important in family traumas of separation and divorce, traumas that are more difficult than bereavement because they take longer to play themselves out. This role for children will be found in all high divorce countries, including Moslem countries. Sometimes young people will leave school or work to care for a parent who is overstressed during or after divorce. If one had to select for the most mature behavior in a stressed family, not infrequently one might select for the behavior of a child, over that of the adults. More in-depth study of compassion and coping in preadolescent and adolescent children is long overdue.

The materials for such study are already at hand in three contemporary settings, the Russian children's collectives, the Israeli kibbutzim and the OSE homes for Jewish refugee children in France in the late thirties and early forties. Already published work on children in these communities (Bronfenbrenner 1970; Bettelheim 1969; Papanek 1975) happens to focus on how the child is socialized, but because the research has been sensitively and emphatically done, one can look at the same materials from the children's perspective. Thus we discover how much nurturance they themselves give to each other and to the adults in their communities.

In the Soviet Union the original intention was to have children grow up in their own collectives, or "boarding schools." Such a program proved too costly to extend to many children, so instead the emphasis now is on the extended-day school. The difference between these extended-day schools and the care centers of western Europe and North America is that the children are routinely taught to take substantial responsibility for each other and for younger children, and to contribute to the physical maintenance of the community and the growing of its food, to an extent true only of the more experimental schools of Euro-North America. Their rewards and satisfactions are in terms of how well they have assisted the group in its functioning, how well they have helped its weaker members, and how effective their partnership with the adults in the school has been in community tasks. Since adults expect a great deal from the children and young people in these collectives, and do not extend emotional support for failure, even very young children learn to look to each other for moral support (Bronfenbrenner 1970).

In the Soviet setting there are still strong family ties, and most children spend nights and holidays with their families. At the time of the founding of the kibbutzim in Israel there was a deliberate and radical break with traditional family life for the first-generation refugees from Europe. These refugees, as Bettelheim (1969) puts it, did not trust themselves to bring up their children in a new way, shaped as they themselves had been by the intensities of parent-child interaction in the ghettos of Europe.

While there is great diversity in practice from one kibbutz to another, and the kibbutzniks represent only a small fraction of the population of Israel, the utopian design of the children's communities is sufficiently unique in concept to have created a new type of personality and world view in the children growing up in them. The designers of these communities, and to a lesser extent the children who have grown up in them, have provided significant social leadership for the national society. In the pattern described by Bettelheim (perhaps uncommon now in 1977) the newborn moves into the infant's house when four days old, and from then on has a visiting relationship only, with parents and siblings. The peer group in the children's houses, age-graded from toddlers through teens, becomes the primary group. Even the infants seem to provide comfort to each other from neighboring cribs. The metapelets, or child-tenders, work in shifts so children do not have a sustained intimate relationship with any adult. With each new age grade they change houses, and toys and objects of every kind belong to the house, not to individual children. The children become very supportive of one another and very independent of adults. While Bettelheim points out the drawbacks to the system, in that the group becomes so highly valued that nonconformity cannot be tolerated, the impressive fact remains that children can do a great deal on their own and for each other, without a primary parenting figure present. What is missing in that setting is intimate one-to-one relationships between children and adults, but the children pull their share of the load in the hardworking agricultural community, and thus are an important support to the adults in it.

The third community no longer exists, and one prays that such a community will never need to exist again. The several hundred children ranging in age from three to fifteen who found their way across Europe to the OSE homes, set up originally by a group of Russian and Polish doctors to save Jewish children, are an incredible testimony to the courage, wit and emotional maturity of those we call children, when put under great stress. The saga of Emil Geisler, the thirteen-year-old boy who brought himself and a six-year-old girl safely to an OSE home in Versailles from across the German border when his parents were taken to a concentration camp, in the face of every danger and with no more information to guide him than a scrap of paper bearing the words, *Maison d'Enfants, Villa Helvetia, Montmorency pres Paris,* can stand for countless others. These children helped one another, patiently rebuilt their environment every time they had to flee to a new location, and helped to cheer the adults when they became discouraged. It is a humbling experience to read the accounts of these children by the director of the OSE program, Ernst Papanek. He had the grace not to underestimate his charges, but to treat them as his partners in the struggle to survive.

Indeed, the materials for a study of children as partners in the human enterprise are at hand. They have only not been utilized.

CHILDREN AND YOUTH AS SHAPERS OF THE FUTURE

The prolongation of childhood and dependency that the extension of school years has brought about in industrialized countries has led to a gradual forgetting on the part of adults about the roles that children and youth have always played in social change. Many of these have been tragic roles, such as in the Children's Crusades. Yet the quality of thought and action that has gone into the protest movements of children and youth should not be judged by their outcomes. Society has never welcomed the fresh insights of its youngest members, nor respected the solitude they need, as much as adults do, for creative thought (Boulding 1962). Bernard Thomas' historically well-researched, sensitive and moving account of the Children's Crusade through the eyes of its young shepherd leader, already old through suffering at the age of twelve, includes an encounter between the shepherd Etienne and the Bishop of Paris. The Bishop speaks:

> Tu prétends, mon enfant, servir mieux que nous l'ordre de la nature qui est voulu par Dieu, dit-il, Mais tu te trompes. Car il est dan l'ordre que les parents commandent aux petits, que les prêtres bénissent, que les chevaliers combattent, que les paysans labourent et que les enfants obéissent. Si nous laissons les enfants prêcher et commander, ne vois-tu pas que l'ordre est inversé? Le diable t'a tendu un piège et tu y es tombé (1973:162-63).

And yet it was the children who saw the futility of the military campaigns, who saw the human waste, and who wanted to try another way. Children and young people were active in all the chiliast peasant uprisings of the Middle Ages, and in the Millennialist and perfectionist movements that ran like a bright thread through all the political and religious upheavals of the Reformation and Counter-Reformation. They swelled the band of Quaker preachers who travelled up and down England and Europe and later the American colonies in the sixteen and seventeen hundreds. Fourteen was not young to be a prophet and visionary and to preach a better life in those centuries.[15]

Fourteen was not young to be a peace activist in the nineteen sixties, either. I had occasion several years ago in a study of children as change agents (Boulding 1972) to compare popular literature about peace containing observations by writers, philosophers and statesmen of the European West (with some Plato, Cicero and Vergil thrown in),[16] with writings of children between the ages of six and seventeen.[17] I found that eighty percent of the entries in the adult book were either rhetorical or vague, contentless statements — not untypical of adult writing on this subject. The entries in the children's book showed a grasp of peace as process, of the conditions of peace, of what must be done to have peace. How would one describe the state of cognitive development or socio-moral maturity of eight-year-old Allison March, who wrote:

> Peace is a word that is
> more said than heard.
> Before you say peace,
> think about it.
> If you really know what
> you are saying, say it.
> But if you don't, why
> say it? (Weiner 1971:107).

The young adult protest movement fought in Europe and the United States for the right to have high school chapters of the college-age radical social change organizations. Discovering they had no freedom of association in their schools, they sometimes turned to civil liberties organizations for help in legal battles. In Des Moines, Iowa in December of 1965, three school children wore black armbands to their respective junior and senior high schools to mourn those who had died in the Vietnam War and to support an extension of the Christmas truce. The students were suspended from school for this symbolic act and with the help of the Civil Liberties Union fought the case to the United States Supreme Court. Four years later the Supreme court handed down an opinion in support of the rights of students (and teachers) to free speech and dissent (Allen 1977:66). Shortly before the Iowa incident, elementary, junior high and senior high young people of Ann Arbor, Michigan (my own five children included) undertook a three-day fast while wearing armbands at school proclaiming "I'm hungry for peace in Selma and Vietnam." The initiative began among high school students, percolated down to younger brothers and sisters. Alarmed parents, certain their children would drop dead from starvation before the three days were over, learned a lot that week. So did school officials. The elementary age children who participated in that fast were among the organizers of Youth Liberation of Ann Arbor by the time they were in junior high school. (See, *Youth Liberation Program* published by this group in the appendix.)

Teenagers were, and still are, present in all the community based movements to create alternative structures — the free schools, the people's clinics, the refuges for children who do not wish to live with their parents. In Denmark children of eight years of age initiated a children's rights movement, and gained the support of adults (Rochefort 1976: 65). Denmark and Norway both have children's refuges with children taking some autonomous responsibility. In the United States, high school and college young people went to the 1971 White House Conference on Children and Youth and published monority reports on every topic, to counteract the protectionist line of the official proceedings. Little attention was paid to them, but they did it anyway.[18] These are the protesters who stay in the system. The teenager protest dropouts enter a hardworking counterculture very different from the drug counterculture. They will be found in politically oriented communes with slightly older young people, in all purpose communes of people of all ages, or in community residential centers supported for this growing category of youth by friendly community people in the cities of Europe and the United States. They often postpone high school accreditation indefintely — they are too busy.[19]

In New York City a Childhood City Directory is now published (Environmental Psychology Program, CUNY, 1977) which lists persons working for and with children and young people to enable them to participate with dignity in city life. The same group also publishes a newsletter. There are probably networks of people committed to working with children in this way in many cities, but the networks are invisible to the general public. There are hopeful signs. The younger generations do not need to struggle alone.

YOUTH ACTIVISM ON THE WORLD SCENE

Because youth are generally seen as self-absorbed in their own youth culture, and, as pointed out, tend to be lumped together with children as nonpersons in the civic sense, I am emphasizing in this section the kinds of roles that youth have played in national and international civic arenas. The difference between what youth can do and what children twelve and under can do is chiefly a matter of accumulated life experiences. Children have far more highly developed civic capacities than they are given credit for, but they do not yet have a large enough experience stock, with some notable exceptions, to engage in the type of activities to be described. While the individuals and groups mentioned here are indeed exceptions, they are perhaps only so because a combination of circumstances, supportive colleagues in the adult world and highly developed natural abilities enabled them to do the things they have done. The ability to take such initiatives and responsibilities exists in countless of their peers who live more ordinary, unexciting lives. Society has few expectations of this age group, and therefore they generally have few expectations of themselves.

University age youth, many still legally minors, have their own international communications networks. Their activities for peace and social justice in the late sixties rocked the world community.[20] While their actions are less dramatic now, their international institution building goes on. Young people in the student category have a long tradition, probably going back to the very inception of the institution of the academy of learning in the first millennium B.C., of social innovation. Sometimes it is highly visible, sometimes it is unnoticed and unsung. The concept of extension work among rural folk by trained agriculturalists, a key factor in modern agricultural productivity, was often begun by young people with a feeling for their own roots in the countryside. It happens that in the United States documentation for that exists. In the state of Iowa a college undergraduate laid the groundwork for a state extension service in 1905 by going out all over the state with a group of five fellow-students to talk to farmers about seed corn (Schulz 1975).

In our time, few people are aware that the institutions of the United Nations University and of the United States Peace Corps are in part the product of student activity in the late 1950's and early 1960's. College students from various campuses across the Unites States formed a group in 1960 known as Americans Committed to World Responsibility which was responsible for the first drafts of the documents which led to the establishment of the Peace Corps by President Kennedy. A subgroup within the ACWR linked with their European counterparts and visited UNESCO to lobby for a United Nations University. The book by Michael Zweig, then an ecomonics student and member of ACWR on The Idea of a United Nations University (1967; edited by Harold Taylor, who aided the group) was a significant step in the long process of formation of the United Nations University that was finally established in 1967 in Tokyo. OXFAM was started by university students in England. A number of international and national relief and community service activities were student initiated in the fifties and sixties. The trail to the youthful initiators of many important international developments becomes oblitereated when adults take over. There are no young people on the United Nations University Council, for example, today.

It would be false to paint a picture of all youth as active shapers of the future. In the large-scale UNESCO study of images of the world in the year 2000 (Ornauer *et al.*1976), undertaken at the height of the student movement in Europe between 1966 and 1968, there was relatively little difference between the views of the youth (fifteen to twenty-six) and adults (twenty-seven to forty) except that the young had a more somber pessimism about the future. Important differences emerged between countries, but not between age groups, a useful reminder that all ages are shaped by the societies they live in.

Given the tendency for the traces of youthful activism to disappear from public consciousness, what happens to young activists when they reach their late twenties? An important recent comparative study of adults who were students at the centers of activism in the early 1960's in Japan and in the United States (Fendrich and Krauss 1977) suggests that students who were active in the civil rights and peace movements of those times have continued to be activist and politically aware in the seventies. Fendrich and Krauss conclude that it was the experience of activism itself that socialized them into continuing roles of political involvement. The common view that these young activists became the disappointed dropouts of the seventies was not supported by this research.

The character of youth activism has changed, but the amount of activism is probably the same or somewhat increased, according to UNESCO reports (United Nations 1977d, 1972a, 1972b, and 1974d). There are radical networks that have separated themselves out from the mainstream of youth activity and the international underground press has been an important bond for these groups. There is also a growing number of associations and activities geared to specific social problems, such as will be described in the next section.

Many mainstream children's and youth organizations are run by professional adults on behalf of youth, but young people's developing skills or organization are beginning to make a new and more visible role for them in their own right, as we shall see below. Young people have begun systematically to attend all United Nations' Conferences and make their own reports. A Symposium on the Participation of Youth in the Second United Nations Development Decade was held in the fall of 1971 in Geneva, and the United Nations pamphlet "Youth in the Second Development Decade" (1972c) has laid out specific and highly useful guidelines for United Nations involvement of youth in planning and development. Action lags far behind words, but at the least words are there.

UNESCO has taken youth very seriously in recent years. In 1972 it published a major study, "Rights and Responsibilities of Youth" (United Nations 1972b), and held an International Youth Seminar in

Poland on Youth, Peace and Education (United Nations 1972a). In 1973 it held a seminar on youth and the use of drugs in industrialized countries in which young people participated (United Nations 1974c). In 1974 it held a seminar on "Groundwork to formulate a policy for youth activities in the population field" (United Nations 1974b), again with youth participating. In 1976 there was a symposium of young workers on the quality of work and work prospects, organized with the help of the ILO and several international trade unions (United Nations 1976d). In 1976 UNESCO did a study of young migrant workers (United Nations 1976a). In 1977 UNESCO has just produced a new study of Youth Institutions and Services: present state and development (United Nations 1977d).

In 1973 UNITAR published "International Youth Organizations and the UN" (Andemicael and Murdock 1973) to add to the documentation of participatory potential of young people. The United Nations Commission on Human Rights has also taken up the role of youth in the deliberations of United Nations bodies, and is considering the appointment by youth organizations in each country of a youth correspondent with the United Nations for issues related to human rights. Its commitment to "development of youth projects with the purpose of identifying and examining situations where the human rights of young people are being seriously restricted or violated" (Resolution XXXII on the Role of Youth in the Promotion and Protection of Human Rights, thirty-second Session of the Commission on Human Rights), is the opening wedge for consideration of many of the issues raised in this study. It came about on the initiative of young people themselves. They are not asking for protection, but for participation.

The following observations from the 1974 UNESCO General Conference Report on The Situtation of Youth will be quoted as representing one type of world overview of youth attitudes today:

> Whether young people are acting within youth movements and political groups or on a less organized basis in small groups, usually without much of a structure, the dominant characteristic of their activities is a rejection and condemnation of the hyposcrisy exemplified in the gulf separating the authorities' statements of intent from the actual achievements. This adamant refusal to compromise, which is an abiding characterisitic of youth reemerges in their struggle for justice, peace and the defense of individual and collective freedoms, and in their striving after an authentic cultural development which is deeply rooted in the real life of different peoples or social milieux . . . .

Thus a change has come about in the nature of dissent as a result of the growing importance, particularly in North America and Europe, of the libertarian trend symbolized by the"hippie" movement. The ultimate goal, as with political groups, is to change society, but the means are different and the social ideal advanced is of a radically different kind. Power is not "at the end of a rifle-barrel" but something to be won for oneself or to be improvised as a parallel alternative to the official system in order to achieve a better life here and now.

It should be pointed out here that among young people in the developing countries the general background of opposition to the Western world means that the distinctively Western forms of dissent are rejected, since they cannot readily adopt forms of dissent which are based solely on improving or repudiating the consumer society to their own situation. For their part they concentrate on such subjects as the political and economic independence of their country, the rejection of cultural colonization, or the development of relations of genuine equality between nations (United Nations 1974d:2,6).

CHILD AND YOUTH-RELATED
NON-GOVERNMENT ORGANIZATIONS

Because the experience worlds of adults and the young are so different, very few adults have first-hand knowledge of the types and extent of participation of children and youth in formal organizations. The documentation of this participation however provides some of the best evidence we have for the degree of assumption of civic roles by those we call children. It happens that the documentation on youth-related transnational non-governmental organizations is available annually in the *Yearbook of International Organizations* published by the Union of International Associations. The organizations listed in this Handbook are the ones that have surfaced in the international community of the many local and national clubs and associations to be found on every continent. Most of these organizations began in one country and spread through the initiative of traveling adults or students. For an organization to be counted as a transnational NGO (nongovernmental organization) it must have sections in at least three countries and an independent international headquarters not financed by any government.

The material to follow may seem somewhat overwhelming to readers not familiar with the world of NGOs. The tables offered should be thought of as data for a whole new set of maps of the international system of the planet. We have world maps showing nation states, and all

Table 7A. Adult NGOs Focused on Services to Children and Youth

Orientation		World Coverage	
Religious, Professional	1	Regional	3
Religious, General	3	International	26
Secular, Professional	14		
Secular, General	11		
TOTAL	29		29

SOURCE: Yearbook of International Organizations, 1974.

kinds of special maps showing the distribution of resources and organized human activities considered important to humankind. There are other kinds of maps we could make but do not — maps for example showing the distribution of the over 3000 transnational nongovernmental organizations that link human beings across national boundaries in a great variety of interests and common purposes ranging from economic and political to educational, cultural and religious. The map least likely to be visualized by people who like to conceptualize the world in terms of maps is the map that shows the distribution of the 103 transnational nongovernmental organizations that link children and youth across national boundaries according to their varied common interests and purposes. This is the undrawn map, the invisible backdrop, to all the data presented in Tables 7A to 7D.

To get the most from these tables, the reader will need to study Appendix 2 which gives the full names of the organizations listed by initials only in the tables. Once the letters become meaningful names, it will further be necessary to use the imagination as actively as possible in constructing mental images of young people engaged in activities corresponding to the labels in the tables, in varying numbers of countries for each organization. Draw on your own childhood memories, your observations of the more active young people you know, and also draw on your daydreams for the planet. One note of realism must be injected into your fantasies, however. As is the case with adult NGOs, it is the "haves" who participate. Poor children will not be found in these NGOs. At the leadership level, the young people who themeselves actively travel the transnational networks their organizations represent are a kind of elite. Nevertheless, they open doors and symbolize opportunity for their less mobile brothers and sisters.

Now for the task of visualizing the NGO world of children and youth: The organizations included in these tables are all taken from listings in the *1974 Yearbook of International Organizations.* The 1974 *Yearbook* lists the organizations to be found in Tables 7A to 7D. The list of child and youth NGOs is not complete because not all such organizations register with the Union of International Associations in Brussels, which publishes the *Yearbook,* but it is as complete as possible. We note first of all that a number of organizations focusing on children and youth are adult professional associations. They are *not* youth organizations but they are interesting to take account of as background information on the tendency of adults to organize the world of childhood and youth. Table 7A gives a numerical overview only, of the twenty-nine NGOs in this category.

Children's NGOs

NGOs geared primarily to the adolescent and early teen years are sex-segregated and happen to all be primarily scouting type organizations run by adults for children. Table 7B lists these NGOs, which are interesting primarily as evidence for the potential transnational experiences they can offer young people. This is particularly true for scouting with its over 100-country networks for girls and boys. The emphasis in these organizations is partly sports, partly civic and character-building, and partly religious. While adult leadership is strong, the teaching emphasis is on self-reliance, with a certain amount of military-style obedience thrown in. It is not until we get to youth and student organizations,

Table 7B. NGOs for Children and Youth for One Sex Only

Name of NGO a	Religious	Secular	Purpose	Number of National Sections
A. NGOs for Girls				
WAGGS		x	Promotion of Scouting	99
ICGS	x		Welfare of Feminine Youth	28
GB	x		Religious Maturity	40
IAPESGW		x	Sports	58
B. NGOs for Boys				
BSWB		x	Promotion of Scouting	104
BB	NO INFORMATION			

SOURCE: Yearbook of International Organizations, 1974.

aSee Appendix for full name of each organization.

however, that we really begin to tap the possibilities of autonomous transnational participation of young people.

Youth and Student NGOs

The forty-four youth organizations shown in Table 7C are to be distinguished from the student organizations in Table 7D by the fact that the young people in the youth organizations will to a considerable extent already be in the labor force, although of the same age as university students. Four of these organizations are associations for young farmers, and four are trade-union related. The fourteen political associations range all the way from socialist to conservative. The religious associations are partly also service, recreational and travel opportunities and thus overlap somewhat with the seventeen associations that facilitate travel for young people. The fact that twelve of the forty-three are religious organizations is a reflection of the fact that the organizing capabilities of religious institutions were more highly developed than any other type of institution at the time of emergence of NGOs. It does not necessarily indicate predominance of adult leadership, since there have been Christian "activist" youth in every century.

The range of activities of the associations of working youth is wide, and indicates that university education is by no means necessary to the development of cultural, social and political interests and international affiliation. These associations have national sections ranging in number from 4 to 115. While some of them may rely on adult administrators, the majority of them probably have significant youth leadership. Founding dates go back to 1909, with six organizations formed before World War II. The remaining thirty-seven were founded since 1945. This means that three to four successive generations are represented in the youth NGOs, over a period of seven decades. If we count the average length of involvement in a youth organization as four years, there have been seventeen "generations" of international youth leadership and collaborative activity.

The earliest of these organizations have links with both the socialist world youth movement and the Christian world youth movement of the previous century. A continous tradition of concern with domestic politics and international affairs for youth clearly antedates both world wars. The organizations are more or less equally divided between regional and international, with Europe, not surprisingly, the best represented in regional organizations. The amount of transnational communication and decision-making represented among these organizations varies greatly, but there is a significant potential here.

Table 7C. NGOs For Youth

Name of NGO[e]	ORIENTATION		International Relations, Political Affairs	Youth Travel Exchange	PROGRAM EMPHASES					SCOPE		Year Founded	Number of Countries
	Religious	Secular			Worker Youth	Rural Youth	Temperance	Sports	Conservation	Regional	International		
CDYLA	1		1							1		1959	17
CENYC	1	1		1						1		1963	13
EYCE		1		1						1		1968	—
EECSCUY		1		1						1		1957	6
ECYF4HC		1				1				1		1965	15
ECYH		1		1						1		1951	—
EUYCD	1		1	1							1	1950	19
FIYTO		1		1							1	1948	24
WAY		1		1							1	1961	62
IBTYE		1		1							1	1958	30
ICCAM		1			1						1	1947	26
IPM-SEI		1			1						1	—	15
JCSFO		1								1		1962	—
IGTYF		1					1				1	1957	9
ILF		1						1			1	1954[b]	26
IMCARY	1					1					1	1923	37
IUSY		1	1								1	1962	61
IUYCD	1		1								1	1945	39
IYCW	1				1						1	1956	74
IYFESC		1							1		1	1932[c]	16
IYHF		1		1						1		1958	44
LCATUYO-EEC		1			1[d]	1[d]				1		1952	6
LEY		1	1							1		1954	7
MEGTYC		1					1			1		—	4
NLRY		1	1							1		—	4
NUYC		1	1							1		—	4
NCIGTYF		1					1			1		1909	4
SJYF	1		1							1		1918	25
SEL		1		1							1	1941	16
ULAEY	1			1						1		—	—
WFY		1	1								1	—	—

Table 7C (cont'd)

Name of NGO	ORIENTATION		PROGRAM EMPHASES							SCOPE			
	Religious	Secular	International Relations, Political Affairs	Youth Travel Exchange	Worker Youth	Rural Youth	Temperance	Sports	Conservation	Regional	International	Year Founded	Number of Countries
WFCY	1			1							1	1926	42
WFDY		1	1									1945	115
WFLRY		1	1								1	1947	22
WOYE		1		1							1	1938	40
CCDYC	1		1									1964	8
PAYM		1	1							1		1962	41
ECBIYO		1		1						1		—	—
IFCPYC		1		1						1		1961	29
EFLRY	1		1	1							1	1970	15
CYE		1								1		—	—
CYCHE		1							1	1		—	—
IYCHE		1							1	1		—	—
ICCS	1	1		1						1	1	1948	35
TOTAL	12	31	14	17	4	3	3	1	3	23	20		

Total Number of Associations: 44
Mean Number of National Sections for 36 Associations reporting: 26.6
Range of Founding Dates: 1909 to 1970

[a] Student organizations excluded

[b] Date of original association; name changed 1946

[c] Name changed 1946

[d] Note this is both a labor organization and a rural one

[e] See appendix--for the full name of each organization

Source: _Yearbook of International Organizations_, 1974.

Table 7D Student NGOs

Name of NGO[b]	ORIENTATION		PROGRAM	EMPHASES			SCOPE		Year Founded	Number of Countries
	Religious	Secular	Profes-sional	Social Service, Student Welfare Exchanges	Education, Evangalism, Reform	International Relations, Political Affairs	Regional	Inter-national		
ARMSA		1	1					1	1966	9
BIRSH		1		1			1		1965	33
CEESA		1	1					1	1965	8
IAESTE		1		1				1	1948	41
IAAS		1	1					1	1957	12
IADS		1	1					1	1951	28
IASBF		1	1					1	1948	51
IFMSA		1	1					1	1951	51
IFNAES		1	1					1	1954[a]	11
IFYM		1	1					1	1945[a]	44
IFES	1				1			1	1947	39
IPSF		1	1					1	1949	23
ISMUN		1				1		1	1948	47
IUS		1		1				1	1946	88
IUSA		1	1					1	1963	--
IVSA		1	1					1	1953	--
IYCSI	1			1				1	1946	60
PRIMCS	1				1			1	1921	70
UESA		1				1	1		1962	--
WSCF	1				1			1	1895	43
WUJS	1			1			1		1924	34
APDSA		1	1				1		--	--
FAMSA		1	1					1	1968	26
SATA		1		1			1		1968	19
WASU		1				1	1		1925	--
TOTAL	5	20	13	6	3	3	6	19		

Total Number of Associations: 25
Mean Number National Sections for 20 Associations Reporting: 36.9
Range of Founding Dates: 1895 to 1965

[a] Successor to earlier association
[b] See appendix—for full name of each organization

Source: Yearbook of International Organizations, 1974.

The twenty-five student organizations shown in Table 7D appear to be fairly evenly divided between associations concerned with furthering their own participation in their chosen professions, and those concerned with social issues and student welfare. While the rate of participation of women in either the youth or the student organizations is not known, one might guess that the same proportion of women are found in these organizations as are found among students studying abroad, which is over twenty percent. The country coverage of the associations ranges from eight to eighty, and the oldest among them, the World Student Christian Federation, was founded in 1895. Pax Romana, the Catholic youth peace and social concerns movement, the World Union of Jewish Students and the West African Students Federation all go back to the 1920s. Though the transnational student movement had its early roots in religious institutions, only one-fifth of the current total of twenty-five associations are religious in orientation, compared with over one-quarter for the youth organizations. The bulk of student associations, twenty-one of the twenty-five, have been founded since 1945. Student movements have close to a century of experience in functioning transnationally, and have taken on new forms to meet new conditions.

Table 7E summarizes the overall picture for youth-related NGOs. That there are twenty-nine adult NGOs focused on youth gives a sense of the importance of youth to professional planners, educators and social service specialists. That there are sixty-eight youth organizations with varying degrees of youth autonomy and self-management, with international networks covering anywhere from forty to one hundred and fifteen countries, suggests how seriously we have underestimated the actual participation of youth in contemporary society. Those who participate in NGOs at the international level represent a socioeconomic elite in their respective countries, and this is equally true of youth and adults. This is therefore not a representative sampling of world youth, nor does it adequately include the radical wing of international youth leadership. Nevertheless, this is what is enumerated, and it cannot serve as the base for the more grassroots-oriented type of activity youth are increasingly involved in. What is needed now is a thorough study by the young people active in the NGO networks, of the activities and ways of working of these sixty-eight youth networks and others that they can uncover.

Two other categories of youth participation should be taken account of in assessing involvement of youth in basic socioeconomic processes domestically and internationally. One includes youth service programs, both compulsory and voluntary, the other consists of youth studying abroad.

Table 7E. All Youth-Related NGOs, Summary Table

```
NGOs for Adults Working with Youth    29
NGOs for Girls                         4
NGOs for Boys                          2
NGOs for Youth                        43
NGOs for Students                     25


Total NGOs for Youth, Adult Managed and Sex Segregated  6
Total NGOs for Aults Working with Youth                29
Total NGOs for Youth, Not Sex Segregated               68

Total Child and Youth-Related NGOs           103
```

SOURCE: Yearbook of International Organizations (1974).

Youth service, under other names, is an old tradition in many folk societies. Young people's groups are part of the social structure of village life, and when they are not working on family land they work in groups, carrying out projects for the village or for themselves, or helping out the widowed. Sometimes young men's and young women's groups work together, although more often they work separately. A modernized version of this tradition in Sri Lanka involves a program of youth farms for young people between the ages of eighteen and thirty years (Ariyaratne 1977:78-98). Earlier traditions of youth work in groups find expression not only in youth farms but in youth cooperatives which are essentially "free enterprise" group farms organized by youth. Some people stay in cooperatives, others move on to their own farms. Twenty years ago a group of high school students in Sri Lanka created the Sarvodaya Shramadana Movement to get to know the rural parts of their own country better. The meaning of the movement's name is "the awaking of all in society by the mutual sharing of one's time, thought and energy." Twenty years later the movement has spread to over 1,200 village communities in Sri Lanka and has an international headquarters. Sri Lankan young people have uniquely bridged the gap between rural and urban life that exists in every country today, by learning traditional skills and sharing new knowledge with villagers, in a continuous movement of youth around all parts of the country. For each such program which receives international fame there are thousands which operate in an entirely local way as part of the daily life of a village.

The traditon of youth work groups is twice blessed in every society. It becomes a setting in which young people learn to exercise the skills of their society with status, dignity and a certain amount of the freedom, and at its best it provides a continuing source of new energy and ideas for the adult society, as well as needed community services. When the work group tradition is taken over by the government of a modernizing country it may or may not keep the special characteristics of autonomy. There is always the danger that over-programing will destroy youth initiatives. At the same time, new resources become available to young people when such programs are nationalized.

It is not clear how many countries have compulsory youth service programs, but the eight country survey undertaken by the United Nations (United Nations, 1975c) shows what a major contribution to community development programs youth provides in countries with large-scale work brigades and service teams consisting of young people. They may be paramilitary in organization, as in Kenya, but perhaps more important is the fact that a few countries have mounted major national development programs utilizing the youngest part of their labor force. The United Nations survey covers Ethiopia, Philippines, Kenya, Chile, Yugoslavia, Lebanon and the United Kingdom. In each case it is clear that successful operation of these programs involves participation of young people in the planning. Yugoslavia, with its self management philosophy, perhaps does the best in fostering planning activities among the young workers themselves.

The voluntary service programs for youth that have developed in the industrialized world also have their roots in older traditions of community service, and are also exposed to both the strengths and the weaknesses of governmental and intergovernmental bureaucracies. The periodically publicized tension between peace corps volunteers and the peace corps as a governmental agency in the United States reflects the inevitable strain that is put on young people when their individual styles of service must be trimmed to fit governmental constraints.

There are various organizations assisting young people to enter voluntary service programs. The International Secretariat for Volunteer Service (ISVS) which performs a linking function for many of these organizations, has published a World Statistical Directory of volunteer and development service organizations (ISVS 1973) based on 1973 data. Tables 8A and 8B give a picture of the extent of involvement of volunteers in service programs around the world based on ISVS data, which includes United Nations volunteer services. The directory also provides detailed information on service programs by country, but only regional and world totals will be reported here. Table 8A shows the regional distribution of long and short-term volunteers, showing how many work domestically and how many go abroad, and table 8B shows

Table 8A. Classification of ISVS Volunteers by Length of Service and Country of Origin, by Region, in 1973

Region of Origin	National[a]		Export[b]	
	L-T[c]	M-T[d]	L-T[c]	M-T[d]
Africa	43806	35450		
America, Central & South	13546	32051	6	72
America, North	7337	28745	8556	1410
Asia	37929	148937	693	12
Australia & Oceania		10	227	43
Caribbean	2586			
Europe	108	4233	14436	332
International[e]			4	3
TOTAL	105312	249426	23922	1872
TOTAL L-T & M-T	354738		25794	
WORLD TOTAL / TOTAL MONDIAL / TOTAL MUNDIAL		380532		

[a] Volunteers working in their own country

[b] Volunteers working abroad

[c] Long-Term, Over 1 year

[d] Medium-Term, 6 weeks to 1 year

[e] Excludes volunteers under ISVS (Int 5) and UNV (Int 7) who are already accounted for within their region of origin.

SOURCE: ISVS (1973).

the fields of service. The world total of 380,532 is inevitably only a part of the actual total, but is as complete as current data collecting mechanisms permit. It will be noted that third world regions export few or no volunteers; their skilled voluntary labor is needed at home. Most "exported" volunteers come from Europe and North America, but many volunteers in this region also choose to work in their own country. Table 8B shows us that over half of the total work programs (see the last

Table 8B. Classification of ISVS Volunteers by Length of Service and Field or Work, in 1973; World Totals Only

	Percentage of volunteers						
	National[a]		Export[b]		National[a]	Export[b]	
Field of work	L-T[c]	M-T[d]	L-T[c]	M-T[d]	total	total	Total[e]
Administration/ business	---	0.2	4.5	13.3	0.1	5.3	0.3
Agriculture	20.8	13.4	11.2	4.0	15.5	10.5	15.3
Community development/ social work	15.5	66.5	12.0	24.9	52.4	13.2	50.8
Education	45.2	14.8	28.2	6.1	23.1	26.2	23.2
Emergency relief	1.2	0.2	---	0.4	0.5	0.1	0.5
Engineering	0.7	0.4	9.2	4.5	0.5	8.8	0.8
Health	11.9	1.9	19.9	40.6	4.6	21.7	5.4
Vocational training	3.5	1.0	5.2	1.4	1.7	4.9	1.8
Misc. Economic/ Social/Cultural	1.0	1.2	8.4	4.5	1.2	8.0	1.5
Misc. Technical/ Scientific	0.2	0.4	1.3	0.3	0.4	1.3	0.4
TOTAL	100.0	100.0	100.0	100.0	100.0	100.0	100.0

[a]Volunteers working in their own country

[b]Volunteers working abroad

[c]Long-Term, Over 1 year

[d]Medium-Term, 6 weeks to 1 year

[e]N = 250,238 students. This table excludes the volunteers for whom field of work was not indicated in the replies received.

SOURCE: ISVS (1973).

column in the table) are in community development and social work. The next most important categories are education and agriculture, with health, vocational training and miscellaneous economic/social/cultural activities accounting for the bulk of the remaining voluntary work. These are world totals, and in any given country the proportions could be very different. Who are the volunteers? Age of entry into volunteer programs varies from twelve to eighteen. Sometimes no upper age limit is set,[21] sometimes it is set at twenty-five. In general, we can assume that the bulk of these volunteers are in their teens and early twenties, doing

Table 9A. Foreign Students Enrolled by Major Region of Study

Major region of origin	1962 Absolute number	%	1965 Absolute number	%	1966 Absolute number	%	1967 Absolute number	%	1968 Absolute number	%
WORLD TOTAL[a]	266,118	100.0	349,393	100.0	379,678	100.0	403,369	100.0	428,883	100.0
Africa	33,083	12.4	43,476	12.5	45,468	12.0	47,015	11.7	48,067	11.2
America,North	34,849	13.1	44,057	12.6	49,719	13.1	54,706	13.6	58,999	13.8
America,South	17,809	6.7	23,843	6.8	24,912	6.6	27,196	6.7	25,194	5.9
Asia	107,228	40.3	146,460	41.9	159,405	42.0	167,767	41.6	182,445	42.5
Europe & USSR	63,396	23.8	73,647	21.1	78,300	20.6	82,821	20.5	87,919	20.5
Oceania	2,690	1.0	3,316	0.9	3,922	1.0	4,196	1.0	4,362	1.0
Origin unknown	7,063	2.7	14,594	4.2	17,952	4.7	19,667	4.9	21,897	5.1
Arab states	38,259	14.4	60,020	17.2	64.170	16.9	67,389	16.7	71,818	16.7
Latin America	31,625	11.9	40,104	11.5	43,844	11.5	49,525	12.3	48,424	11.3
Developed countries	91,848	34.5	110,125	31.5	119,329	31.4	126,430	31.3	135,542	31.6
Developing countries	167,207	62.8	224,674	64.3.	242,397	63.9	257,272	63.8	277,444	63.3

[a]For countries of study not included see footnote on Table 8A.

SOURCE: United Nations (1973).

Table 9B. Students Abroad by Major Region of Origin

Major region of study	1950 Absolute number	1950 %	1955 Absolute number	1955 %	1960 Absolute number	1960 %	1965 Absolute number	1965 %	1968 Absolute number	1968 %
WORLD TOTAL[a]	107,589	100.0	149,590	100.0	237,503	100.0	349,393	100.0	428,883	100.0
Africa	7,100	6.6	10,331	6.9	18,238	7.7	27,048	7.7	28,555	6.7
America,North	33,873	31.5	42,166	28.2	62,095	26.1	96,623	27.7	143,881	33.5
America,South	8,218	7.6	8,928	6.0	10,549	4.4	15,168	4.3	16,147	3.8
Asia	8,005	7.4	14,091	9.4	23,991	10.1	50,961	14.6	66,907	15.6
Europe & USSR	49,844	46.3	72,012	48.1	117,125	49.3	151,485	43.4	164,665	38.4
Oceania	549	0.5	2,062	1.4	5,505	2.3	8,108	2.3	8,728	2.0
Arab states	8,155	7.6	11,443	7.6	21,210	8.9	40,338	11.5	47,602	11.1
Latin America	9,090	8.4	10,325	6.9	12,286	5.2	17,798	5.1	21,242	5.0
Developed countries	85,713	79.7	118,480	79.2	188,131	79.2	262,947	75.3	324,763	75.7
Developing countries	21,876	20.3	31,110	20.8	49,372	20.8	86,446	24.7	104,120	24.3

[a]Not including 11 countries of study: Brazil, China (mainland), Fiji Islands, German Democratic Republic, Jamaica, Democratic People's Republic of Korea, Peru, South Africa, Southern Rhodesia, Venezuela, Democratic Republic of Viet-Nam, for which data are not available.

SOURCE: United Nations (1971b).

Table 9C. Female Foreign Students in Relation to Total Foreign Students Enrolled

Major regions of study	1962	1965	1966	1967	1968
WORLD TOTAL[a]					
Female as % of Total Foreign Students Enrolled	18.5	19.7	20.6	21.0	21.7
AFRICA					
Female as % of Total Foreign Students Enrolled	16.0	13.3	14.2	15.0	15.6
AMERICA, NORTH					
Female as % of Total Foreign Students Enrolled	21.5	21.8	22.9	23.3	24.0
AMERICA, SOUTH					
Female as % of Total Foreign Students Enrolled	20.8	20.4	21.3	19.4	23.1
ASIA					
Female as % of Total Foreign Students Enrolled	21.0	23.0	23.8	24.0	24.8
EUROPE AND USSR					
Female as % of Total Foreign Students Enrolled	16.6	18.8	19.3	19.6	20.0
OCEANIA					
Female as % of Total Foreign Students Enrolled	15.8	17.2	17.4	18.0	18.3
ARAB STATES					
Female as % of Total Foreign Students Enrolled	14.0	12.1	13.5	14.4	14.8
LATIN AMERICA					
Female as % of Total Foreign Students Enrolled	20.7	19.7	20.5	18.2	21.3

[a]In addition to the eleven countries of study listed in the footnote on Table 8A, the following seven countries have not been included in this table as the breakdown of foreign students by sex was not available: Canada, Greece, Guatemala, India, Jamaica, Libya, Uruguay.

SOURCE: United Nations (1971b).

this service before they settle down to a permanent occupation and the establishment of their own families. It is clear that a substantial number of young people are making a concrete contribution to economic and social development domestically and internationally, and are at the same time gaining experience which makes them valuable partners in planning activities at every level.

The last category of youth to be surveyed are those who study abroad. Study abroad is in some ways the opposite of youth service, for the emphasis is on training, and on a suspension of other responsibilities during the training. The story of student movements recorded on the preceeding pages suggests that such a suspension of responsibility in fact does not take place, but that the student is continually and autonomously exploring ways to relate to the larger society of which she is a part. If this is true of students who enter universities in their home country, it is probably even more true of students who go abroad. Set down in a different society for a period of time, the students gain many more angles from which to view society, and thus many more ideas of "what is to be done." The international student movements described earlier are a witness to the results of this kind of exposure. Students are then as important a category to be considered as any other we have looked at.

Tables 9A and 9C indicate numbers of foreign students enrolled by region of study from 1950 to 1968, numbers of students by region of origin, and percent females of all foreign students. While Europe, North America, Oceania have seventy-five percent of all foriegn students in their regions, it is nevertheless worthy of note that 24.3 percent of students choose to study in the third world. This group is partially first world students, partially third world students studying in another country than their own. The percent of women among these students is rising slowly but surely, from 18.5 to 21.7 percent between 1962 and 1968 for the world as a whole.

Presumably, foreign student enrollments have been steadily increasing since 1968, so by the mid-seventies we might estimate over 500,000 students going out each year to study in a country not their own. The knowledge and skills which these young people are gaining in relation to world problems is substantial. When we add the students abroad to the volunteers abroad, we are turning out close to 1 million people every two to four years, most of whom are in their teens and their twenties, who are competent to function in several languages, in several different cultural and socioeconomic settings, and who are nevertheless almost totally excluded from significant participation in planning policy-making either in their own countries or in the United Nations and other international agencies.

For all the involvement of youth in transnational organizations, in service programs and in study abroad, most adults have very little idea what youth think about or do. Yet a surprising amount of information about their thoughts and lifeways is available. In the past decade there have been surveys of the interests, activities, attitudes and opinions of youth in thirty countries, for the most part undertaken with considerable research sophistication. The data from these surveys is available on computer tape from the Roper Public Opinion Research Center which has produced an International Youth Study Inventory (Hastings n.d.). One of the finest statements of the actual and potential contributions to the general welfare of younger people through voluntary service and creative educational ventures is found in Arthur Gillette's "The Young Adolescent: An Untapped Resource" (1974).

Taking into account all the thinker-doer roles we have indentified for children and young people: their work in the labor force, their work in childbearing and rearing, their service and nurturance to their own parents, and their peace and social changes activities nationally and internationally, one might stop and ask, what would happen if all the world's children and youth went on strike? They would have good reason to, and they are more than fifty percent of the world's population.

NOTES

1. In some countries there are special provisions for treatment of criminals under the age of thirty.
2. For an overview of many of the new findings about play, see Mary Reilly's *Play as Exploratory Learning,* 1974. See also Huizinga's classic, *Homo Ludes,* 1955.
3. See Leila Berg's "Moving Toward Self-Government" (1971:9-50) for a further account and references for each of these experiments.
4. A more complete description of these categories will be found in Rogoff et al., 1976:254—257.
5. The definition of work in the sense of economic activity, for statisical purposes, is difficult enough in dealing with the adult male labor force alone. It becomes progressively more difficult in dealing with the female labor force, and most difficult of all in dealing with the child labor force. I will here define a "working" or "economically active" child as one who is engaged in sytematic productive activity on behalf of self or a larger unit household, commune or outside employer, where regular requirements of time input and some measure of output are involved, whether or not the output is renumerated. A child seeking such regular productive activity, or subject to placement by adults who seek work on the child's behalf, but not currently working, may be considered "unemployed" in this context. Economically active children may fall in one of the following categories: 1) self-employed (as employers or own-account workers), 2) employees and 3) unpaid family workers. The line between doing some chores for one's household and being an unpaid family worker may sometimes be difficult to draw, but in general a child should be considered an unpaid family worker if working regularly for a major part of each day at one or more household enterprises.
6. One obvious bit of data which is lacking is the age at which it is legal to work. In some countries, "All persons of ten years of age and over, whether employed or enemployed, are included in the 'economically active population' " (United Nations 1976a:5). Most countries report the work force from age fifteen and up. National legislation and practice are so at variance here, and differ so much from one part of a country to another, that there are no firm figures to report. The fifteenth year can be taken as the general norm for the age at which to begin work.
7. There are currently some efforts to deal with the protection of young

workers. For example, in Costa Rica: By Act No. 4930 17 Nov 71, employers are authorized to employ apprentices in agriculture, who can be thirteen to eighteen years old, subject to authority of Ministry of Labour and National Organization for the Protection of Children. The National Apprenticeships Institute is in charge of the organization and inspection of apprenticeships in all occupations.

In Belgium, by the Employment Act of 16 March 1971, children under fourteen may not be made to work except as actors or performers in cultural or similar events. They may not work over ten hours a day or more than four and a half hours without break of half an hour if the day exceeds four and one half hours, or one hour if it exceeds six hours (*Yearbook of Human Rights*, United Nations, 1971d).

A great many countries are just now in this decade ratifying International Labour Organzation (ILO) conventions protecting children below eighteen from working underground, and ensuring reasonable working conditions.

8. The only three countries reporting conscription for women in 1968 were Israel, Guinea and Mali.

9. There is evidence that the higher the nutritional level, the earlier the onset of fertility, which helps to explain the high proportion of teenage mothers in the United States. Teenage fertility is relatively low, probably nutrition-related, in many third-world countries (Frisch 1978).

10. Shirley Hartley (1975) gives an excellent analysis, based on a variety of cross-cultural data that supplements out of wedlock birth statistics, of the "concatenation" of factors that reduce access to alternative solutions to and increase likelihood of illegitimite births for women in various types of societies.

11. The information in this section is based on "The Status of the Unwed Mother: Law and Practice" (United Nations 1971c). The situation is changing yearly however. The *1971 Yearbook of Human Rights* (United Nations 1971d) reports that Bulgaria became one of the nations recognizing that "children born out of wedlock have equal rights with those born in wedlock" (Constitutional Article 38(4)). The Federal Republic of Germany, Austria, and the Netherlands are also reported (*1970 Yearbook of Human Rights*, United Nations 1970) as moving towards abolition of the distinction between legitimate and illegitimate children, though for the Netherlands "recognition of incestuous children remains impossible."

12. Nizalovszky (1968) comments that ancient cultural traditions can influence modern law, and suggests that old Germanic traditions of making no distinction between births in and out of wedlock are responsible for the "advanced" laws abolishing those distinctions in Scandinavia today. Generally, however, he relates the labeling of illegitimate birth to the capitalist system and its associated practice of treating women and children as property rather than as persons. Hartley (1975) however, points out that tribal law also classifies children born outside accepted contractual arrangements as illegitimate, and sometimes requires the death of the mother and child. Generally, however, it appears that tribal societies have more ways of absorbing illegitimate children into either the mother's or the father's kinship system than industrial societies do.

13. Hartley (1975:71-72) reports studies which match unwed mothers with similar nonpregnant women and find the differences between the two groups are considerably less than earlier research had led investigators to expect.

14. In the West, a bereaved adult can rarely be open and truthful with a child about death. This means that the child has to figure out all alone what has really happened when a relative dies, based on her own observation and the strange concealment behavior of adults, and then be supportive (much as the eighteen-month old was supportive in the earlier quote) of her parents in a period of great grief. What a test of the maturity of a child! It is almost as hard for young adults, for death is often treated as an embarrasment even with older young people. Yet the young not only find ways to cope, but ways to pour out a little extra in the way of responsiveness to those around them.
15. Among the eloquent Quaker preachers of the late sixteen and early seventeen hundreds were William Hunt, aged fourteen, George Newlan, aged twelve, Ellis Lewis, aged thirteen, and Christiana Barclay, aged fourteen (Homan, 1939:79).
16. Peace It's Wonderful (Fenton, 1971).
17. Peace is You and Me. (Weiner, 1971).
18. See Recommendations and Resolutions, White House Conference on Children and Youth, 1971, which published all minority reports as well as regular commision reports. While this in a new way justified the faith of the change-committed youth who attended, the entire conference and monumental-but-never-to-be-read report is an example of token approaches to youth which do not involve taking seriously the careful thinking both mainstream and protest youth did at the conference. It will not be found on best-seller lists, nor referred to in widely read literature on the young.
19. For an analysis of adolescent subcultures from conservative to radical on the American scene, see Boulding (1975).
20. For analysis of student roles in this era, see Califano (1970) and Emmerson (1968).
21. Some United States Peace Corps volunteers are in their sixties, but these are the exception.

II
Children and Youth as Objects:
Protection and Victimization

Now that we have examined in considerable depth the active roles of children and youth as thinkers and doers, and seen to what extent they take the responsibility for the world they live in, we will swing to the opposite perspective and see how few rights they have, because of their "protected" minority status. We are moving from the young person as subject, actor, shaper, of society, to the child as object, the "sheltered" and victimized member of society. In the previous Section I set out to emphasize the competence of the young, and did not detail the limiting factors on that competence deriving from their location in the social structure, and from their lack of of life experience. I did not feel it necessary to dwell on those limitations, because the bulk of literature on children deals with what children cannot do, or with the threshholds between can and can't in the life of the growing child. Neither did I feel it necessary to deal with "bad" children—those who willfully refuse to do what is expected of them. Again, there is plenty of literature on this subject.

In this section, it is the victimage of the young that will be emphasized, and therefore the human resources of the compassion and caring of adults who relate to children as parents, teachers, "helping professionals," employers and friends, that mitigate that victimage, will not be discussed. They are real enough — the human race could not have survived without them. It does not seem plausible to me as socialist theory states, that a transition from capitalism to socialism alone will reduce the victimage of children and youth. While it is true that children in socialist societies benefit from a better distribution of food, education and health care than in most nonsocialist countries, there remains a type of social victimage of children in socialist as well as capitalist societies. Of course, there are compassionate adults and loving families in all types of economic systems who soften the effects of institutional constraints on children. In describing the child and youth as object and victim in this section, I mean to refer to the basic institutional supports for considering the child as immature, incompetent and manipulable for "its" own good. These institutional supports are to be found equally in socialist and capitalist societies. The manipulation is carried out by the state through the legal system, and by the family through custom supported by law.

Each society has its legal underpinnings for this situation. In the Anglo-American world "we inherited a common law concept of status derived from a feudal order which denied children legal identity and treated them as objects or things, rather than as persons"(Foster 1974:8). The universal interests of parents as against the world at large as recognized by law has been succinctly stated by a legal analyst:

> A parent has an interest in his relation with his child. The elements of this interest are three: (1) The industrial *services* received from the child; (2) the social *pleasure* ministered by the child; (3) the chastity of a family self-respect and honor" (Wigmore, Summary of the Principles of Torts, §§ 29—36; Wigmore, Interference with Social Relations, 21 Am. Law Rev. 764†).

In all societies where such rights have not been explicitly removed by the state, the family is a kind of minisovereignty standing over against the state, and subject to the state in strictly limited ways. This gives parents a great deal of power over children.

The basic fact to be emphasized here is that the child is, before the law, *dependent.* Children and youth do not have autonomy of response or decision-making so that they can leave unpleasant or hurtful situations, or choose better ones, even when they are factually capable of making such decisions. The infant and the twenty-year-old alike are considered subject to their parents and the state in ways that the twenty-one year old is not.[1] *This* is what makes them liable to victimage, not their incompetence, which varies among children and youth as it varies among adults, nor systematic ill-will on the part of parents, which is certainly not the prevailing attitude of parents to children. Yet we have seen the necessity to establish the legal autonomy of women in the marriage relationship, even though marriage is supposed to be, and often is, a relationship of mutual love and nurturance. When it is not, women can be severely victimized if they are not free to leave. Similarly with children. While the parent-child relationship is supposed to be, and often is, a relationship of mutual love and nurturance, when it is not, children can be severely victimized if they are not free to leave.

If the concept of "protection" seems to get short shrift in this section, it is not because protection of human beings at their points of vulnerability is not appropriate, but because "protection" and the conditions under which it is carried out need to be much more carefully thought through than has been done to date. The issue of "equal rights" versus "protection" has not yet been adequately clarified for any class of human beings. All human beings have certain vulnerabilities under certain conditions, and need to be protected when they are vulnerable. Class action[2] in protection however ignores individual capabilities and therefore may violate rights of autonomous action. This is true for men, who vary in physical strengths and capabilities, as it is true for women and children. What is being exposed in the material that follows are the dangers of class action protection for children, which frequently leaves them even more vulnerable to precisely that from which society intends to protect them.

This has been a very difficult section to write because I am keenly aware of the dangers of questioning basic understandings about how human beings care for one another in families. The family as a unit of social reproduction providing individualized care and affection for its members of all ages has been a remarkably resilient instrument throughout human history.[3] I expect it to outlast many other social institutions we have come to take for granted, precisely because it individualizes human nurturance, enhances the capacity of human bonding in all other settings, and provides for society's young in ways at once holistic and "economically" efficient. Asymmetric patterns of parenting that leave one parent with the majority of the responsibility for offspring is not inherent in the nature of families, but stems from cultural formulations. The shift from institutional care to foster home care for children who do not have families to care for them, or children endangered by their families, is a recognition of the peculiar effectiveness of the familistic settings for the nurture of the young. The tragedy in many industrialized societies today, as welfare workers well know, is that there are not enough foster families capable of giving adequate nurturance to these hurting children.[4] In my view the same social pathology that denies the personhood of children cripples the emotional maturity of adults so they cannot be adequate parents. The vicious cycle is repeated indefinitely as each generation disqualifies the next for adequate parenthood. Adult-children relationships are among the most precious relationships a society has, and they are in need of repair.

By emphasizing the need for autonomy and emancipation for children and youth in this book, I am not urging the destruction of family life but a serious reconsideration of how to ensure emotional and intellectual maturity in the next generation, and how to ensure that generation's input to the ongoing social process, in order that both family and society can be more healthy and nurturant in the future. False romanticization of The Family will not accomplish this. By urging autonomy and emancipation I am providing no *answers* to these questions. The "how?" remains. In one sense it is ridiculous to separate out children in exploring these social pathologies, because families are tightly interconnected units and much can be done through therapeutic approaches to whole families. This will not work however as long as children are considered second-class beings. As this book is pointing out, social rigidities are such that children suffer when a too simple approach to maintaining the "sanctity of the family" is taken. Therefore the questions raised here must be raised. Because I am an optimist I am confident that in the asking, processes can be set in motion that will provide better futures for children and adults alike.

In the material that follows, we will focus on those aspects of violence-perpetuating intergenerational cycles that impinge most directly on children. We will do this by first looking at physical abuse of children in home and school, then their vulnerability to accident and disease, their malnourishment and maleducation, and finally their status in law. When possible, the same fifteen countries representative of different regions used in Part I will be used for illustration in Part II.

PHYSICAL ABUSE OF CHILDREN AND YOUTH IN HOME AND SCHOOL

Child abuse cannot simply be labeled a disease of civilization, however tempting that might be. While there is much evidence in anthropological literature for gentle loving treatment of children in tribal societies, there is also the widespread fact of infanticide, the only means of birth control available to many societies. There is also the evidence of painful initiatory rites including male and female circumcision (the former, but not the latter, is medically condoned in western societies) and not infrequent reports of societies with a high level of interpersonal and intergenerational violence. Margaret Mead's *Sex and Temperament in Three Primitive Societies* (1950) can serve as a reminder of the range of behaviors of which both sexes are capable when they are systematically socialized in one pattern or another.

Those who perceive civilization as an evolutionary development beyond tribalism, however, are in for a rude shock if they look for better treatment of children in civilizational societies. De Mause writes that

Infanticide of both legitimate and illegitimate children was a regular practice of antiquity, that the killing of legitimate children was only slowly reduced during the Middle Ages . . . Infanticide during antiquity has usually been played down despite literally hundreds of clear references by ancient writers that it was an accepted, everyday occurrence. Children were thrown into rivers, flung into dung-heaps and cesstrenches, "potted" in jars to starve to death, and exposed on every hill and roadside "a prey for birds, food for wild beasts to find" . . . (de Mause 1974:25).

Aristippus claimed

. . .that a man could do what he wants with his children, for "do we not cast away from us our spittle, lice and such like, as things unprofitable, which nevertheless are engendered and bred even out of our own selves . . ." (de Mause 1974:26).

Seneca said

Mad dogs we knock on the head; the fierce and savage ox we slay; sickly sheep we put to the knife to keep them from infecting the flock; unnatural progeny we destroy; we drown even children who at birth are weakly and abnormal. Yet it is not anger, but reason that separates the harmful from the sound (de Mause 1974:27).

Child sacrifice is a practice not reserved to the ancient Carthaginians.

Sealing children in walls, foundations of buildings, and bridges to strengthen the structure was also common from the building of the wall of Jericho to as late as 1843 in Germany (de Mause 1974:27).

The practice of beating children goes as far back as there are written records. Beating instruments in the Age of Enlightenment in Europe included

whips of all kinds, including the cat-o-nine-tails, shovels, canes, iron and wooden rods, bundles of sticks, the discipline (a whip made of small chains), and special school instruments like the flapper, which had a pear-shaped end and a round hole to raise blisters (de Mause 1974:41).

Severe bruising, bloodying and disfigurement were a regular part of a child's life from infancy. De Mause could only find one child out of eighty seventeenth century children whose biographies he studied who was not regularly beaten. In schools, sexual abuse and beating went hand in hand. Quintillian warned Roman parents that beating was associated with sexual abuse and recommended that both be discontinued. The use of infants and small children for sexual satisfaction has evidently always been widespread. Setting unweaned infants at *fellatio* is mentioned by Roman writers (de Mause 1974:45). Anal intercourse with boys of toddler age and on, and raping of very small girls, was all part of the picture, as it is today. Some of this took place in families, some in brothels to which children were sold by their parents, and sometimes a child was sold as a sexual toy to a wealthy individual.

The same set of practices, on a small scale, continues today and is occasionally reported in the press. The latest United Nations Resolution for the Suppression of Traffic in Persons and Exploitation of the Prostitution of Others was passed in 1959. A background paper prepared in 1975 for International Women's Year points out that the international traffic in very young girls and women continues on a much larger scale than is reported to or controllable by INTERPOL (United Nations 1975b). The current publicity in the United States about "chicken porn" films made by adults for adults, showing children engaging in a variety of sexual acts with each other, only makes visible once again a usually invisible activity. It appears from United States research that perhaps as much as twelve percent of reported child abuse, when investigated, turns out to include sexual abuse (Sgroi 1975:18—21).

Dr. Judianne Densen-Gerber, director of the Odyssey Institute, estimates that in New York City alone about 60,000 children — some as young as fourteen months old — are being exploited by pornographers (Densen-Gerber and Ward 1975). (This is a controversial estimate. Others would put it rather lower.)

Many of the children in these productions are runaways who are trapped into pornographic filmmaking and prostitution by unscrupulous operators. In some cases, parents sell their own children's services to pornographic film producers or combine with the children to make such films.

Incest is an important category of sexual child abuse. Current estimates in the United States based on California figures are that there could be as many as 1.3 cases for every 1000 households, or nine per 1,000 girls under eighteen. (These figures might need downward revision for extrapolation to the national scene, given the atypical nature of the California social environment.) (Sudia unpublished memorandum, 1975). Attitudes toward incest, and toward sexual relations between children and adults, varies enormously. On the one hand there is the concern for the effect of pathological sex relationship on children and youth; there are the findings that a high proportion of women in drug abuse programs and in institutions for delinquent girls, have been involved in incestuous relations. (Case studies applying to individual institutions only are available, no national estimates.) At the other extreme there is the children's sexual liberation movement, as represented for example by the Paedophile Information Exchange in England, which exists to promote autonomous sexual relationships between children, and between children and adults.[5] (Moody 1977). A similar movement is apparently developing in the United States.[6] Adults on either side of this issue are equally opposed to sexual exploitation of children by adults, but take the opposite approaches to the problem. The inbetween position is that this is a relatively minor problem in family relations correctable by good and timely family therapy.

Some children's rights advocates agree with the paedophile movement that sex between children, and sex between children and adults, can be "liberating" (Farson 1974:Ch. 9; Holt 1974:Ch. 2). While it is perfectly possible to visualize free, affectionate sexual activity both between children (as noted by various anthropologists) and between adults and children (as noted by Germaine Greer in Farson 1974:151) the conditions under which these activities can be healthy, normal and mutually rewarding need to be very carefully specified, particularly in industrial societies. The very widespread experience of prepubertal rape now being uncovered among adult women who previously never dared to speak of it discloses a level of pain and fear associated with this early sex that itself contributes to the repetitive circle of pathology. See Brownmiller (1975), Russell (1975), Medea and Thompson (1974), Macdonald (1971), Russell and Van de Ven's *Crimes Against Women* (1977) and Sgroi (1975).

The average citizen in an industrialized society in the West does not believe that child abuse exists today except as an extremely pathological, exceptional event, yet the phenomena is forcing itself on the public consciousness. A recent United States policy statement (Broadhurst 1975:23) defines an abused child as any child under age eighteen who

a) has sustained physical injury as a result of cruel or inhumane treatment or as a result of malicious acts by his parent or by any other person responsible for his care or supervision; b) has been sexually molested or exploited, whether or not he has sustained physical injury, by his parent or any other person responsible for his care or supervision.

The state of Florida, which now has the best child abuse reporting system in the United States, had the startling experience of having child abuse reporting increase "from a total of thirty-nine in the two-year period, 1967-68 to 48,814 in the twenty-three month period from November 1971 through September 1973" (Hurt 1975:7) as a result of an intensive public education program designed to alert teachers, doctors and citizens to their responsibilities to report suspected abuse (and neglect, a less violent but potentially equally serious condition). As investigative and family therapy teams are formed state by state to deal with these abuses, the evidence rapidly accumulates on the extent and severity of child abuse practices.[7] Abuse of women, and abuse of the aged, are being uncovered by the same procedures. Estimates for the United States as a whole based on Florida studies suggests that perhaps 91,000 children are abused each year who are never reported (Nagi 1975:15).

Researchers working with child abuse are becoming increasingly concerned that the phenomenon is being overlabelled as a type of "disease" which infects individuals without looking at the broader context, which is a malfunctioning family (or a malfunctioning child care institution). Community programs aimed at helping child-abusing parents who frequently want help in controlling their own behavior are an important resource in reducing child abuse behavior. A whole new approach to child abuse counseling takes the position that the decision for parents and the child to stay together, or for the child to leave the home, must be taken by the family as a whole with adults and the child participating equally in the decision. If the child is simply removed from the home without a prior family process of confronting the issues involved, both the child and the adults bear lifelong burdens of unresolved guilt which impede further development (James Struve personal communication). Certainly this approach gives more recognition to the dignity and the autonomy of the child than a simple removal process, yet does not do so at the expense of the parents. Attention has also been too exclusively focused on abuse of under-twelves, when according to some estimates one third of child abuse in the United States at least, is directed at adolescents over twelve years of age (Gelles, Straus and Steinmetz 1975). This raises important questions about the varying skills of over-twelves in coping with problem families, and has implications for the workability of emancipation rights of over-twelves. This will be further discussed in the section on legal rights.

A recent eight-country study of child abuse and neglect (Kamerman 1975:34-37) surveying Canada, France, West Germany, Israel, Poland, the United Kingdom, Yugoslavia and the United States, sought to find out how abuse and neglect was defined, what protective legislation and policies existed to facilitate reporting and dealing with it, and what research is being carried out on the subject. Yugoslavia does not separate the concept of abuse from the general issue of predelinquency; Poland recognizes the concept, but believes the condition to be negligible. The other countries are reporting increasing awareness of the problem, and are struggling with how to define and how to treat it. The existence of this phenomenon is in a way a critique of existing child welfare programs in countries that pride themselves on their concern for children. It therefore becomes all the more difficult to accept the possibility that new approaches may be required to protect children from abuses so gross that people prefer to believe that they don't exist. One fact should be noted in regard to the perception of child abuse. Once any society takes seriously the possibility that child abuse exists and takes steps to uncover and deal with it, it finds that the condition is far more widespread than anyone, including the pioneers who develop the reporting system, ever anticipated in advance. Given the widespread denial of the problem, we are a long way from being able to develop international consensus on the need for special protection of children against abuse.

A more indirect but in the long run significant approach to the problem is the increasing recognition among human development professionals of the importance of nurturant tactile stimulation of infants and children by adults in the early years of life. Children deprived of affectionate touching are handicapped in establishing warm human relations as adults. As Montague (1971) points out, industrial societies tend to deprive children of this type of stimulation because of impersonal child-rearing practices associated with "modernity." Prescott (1977) goes further and directly relates physical violence in an adult to lack of physical affection from parents in childhood, basing his findings on a study of forty cultures.

The variety of "body contact" techniques developed in the new group therapy movements, in the paedophile movement, and in the gay rights movement, can all be seen as attempts to break through cycles of impersonality and violence. If some of these movements appear extremist, it should be remembered that they have arisen in response to an extreme situation of social violence, of which child abuse is one important part. They provide necessary signals that whole sets of social practices need to be changed if children are to grow up in nonabusive settings.

Most child abuse takes place within families. Since the United Nations is committed, as is every national legal system, to protecting the rights of parents over children, this leaves children very defenseless. A clue as to the prevalence of parental beatings as normal routine (not categorized as child abuse) in the United States is given by a study of middle class college students who were asked whether they had received physical punishment or been threatened with physical punishment during their last year of high school. Fifty-two percent had experienced actual or threatened punishment, and half of that group experienced it *frequently*. A survey of American adults indicated that almost everyone had been spanked as a child, one-third frequently (Steinmetz and Straus 1974:6).

In general, research on the use of physical punishment to control "misbehavior" suggests that this *increases* the level of aggression in the child (Steinmetz and Straus 1974:Part IV). "Violence begets violence, however peaceful and altruistic the motivation" (Steinmetz and Straus 1974:3). It appears, then that much of the pathology of child-adult relations in human society is laid bare in the pain-pleasure-beating-sex syndrome. It has a long history, and will not easily be eradicated.

A very different kind of violence inflicted on children in industrialized societies is the violence of inattention. Parents preoccupied with their own identity crises or their own avenues of escape from reality have little time for listening to and being with children, and the TV syndrome for children is one frequent result. Slogans for adults such as "the child-free family" and "uninterrupted sex" accentuate a social trend toward treating children as intruders. A recent study by the United States Foundation for Child Development of a cross-section of 2,200 seven to eleven-year olds shows how fearful grammar-school children have become, of the world at large.

> . . . two-thirds are afraid that "somebody bad" might get into their houses; a quarter are afraid that when they go outside somebody might hurt them.
>
> Nearly a quarter of the children said they felt afraid of "TV programs where people fight and shoot guns," in an apparent link between TV watching and fear. And heavy watchers, four or more hours a weekday, were twice as likely to feel "scared often." However, it was not clear whether heavy watching cause the fear or was the result of being fearful about going out.
>
> Many children desired more contact with their parents, nearly half wishing their fathers would spend more time with them and more than a third wishing their mothers would (Flaste 1977).

The school, unfortunately, joins with the home in enforcing the pathology of fear. Recent research on corporal punishment in schools (again in the United States) indicates a reversal of recent antibeating trends, with corporal punishment now in use in seventy-four percent of the districts responding to the survey. An oft quoted statistic from the Dallas, Texas school district is that physical punishment was administered over 2000 times in an average month for the 1971-72 school year (Hapkiewicz 1975:2). In a Michigan study it was found that seventy percent of the school superintendents are in the American slang term "jocks" who see a positive value in physical pain as a result of their own athletic experience. Studies of punished children find that they rarely remember what they were punished for (Maurer 1974:619). Psychologists are finding that punishment is not an objective tool in the hands of adults but is administered vindictively, revengefully (Maurer 1974:614-625).

If there is to be a reversal of the practice of corporal punishment in schools, it may come from a tiny island off the coast of Britain. The December 12, 1977 issue of *Behavior Today* reports that

> A fifteen-year old British schoolboy, sentenced to three strokes of the birch by a juvenile court on the Isle of Man, has forced the British government to defend the legality of corporal punishment before the European Court of Human Rights in Strasbourg, France. His contention that the sentence violates the European Convention on Human Rights will probably be upheld by the international tribunal.

De Mause says that "The history of childhood is a nightmare from which we have only recently begun to awaken" (1974:1). He documents an evolutionary shift from infanticide and abandonment through various modes of "shaping" (by physical and moral violence) the child to a recently developing "helping mode." Yet current reports of child abuse make one question whether this helping mode, another label for the protection that the Declaration of the Rights of the Child offers, is such an evolutionary breakthrough. It leaves children at the mercy of their parents, as the persons who are supposed always to act in their offspring's best interests. As we have already seen, and shall see further when discussing the status of children in law, the family can be dangerous to a child, and the child has no escape from it. Legal emancipation for children so they can have independent recourse to outside help may be the only cure for an ancient pathology. Centuries of treating children as objects, a routine implanted in each generation by its parents, will be hard to break.[8]

THE VULNERABILITY OF CHILDREN TO DEPRIVATION AND DEATH FROM DISEASE, INCLUDING MALNUTRITION-RELATED DISEASE, AND ACCIDENTS

Another category of victimage for children does not come from direct infliction of violence, but from the indirect violence stemming from the patterning of social structures that leads to malnutrition, proneness to certain kinds of diseases, and vulnerability to certain types of accidents. The consequences of these institutional patterns can be a permanent stunting of physical and mental growth or other lifetime handicaps such as blindness and crippling, or it can be death in early childhood.

The riskiest time for a newborn human being, as is well known, is the first years of life. Table 10 based on World Health Organization Statistics, shows what a risky thing it is to be born, and how few the chances are of surviving into the second year of life, no matter what the continent on which one is born. Survival chances increase markedly if one lives to age one, and even more markedly if one lives to age four. A child who has survived to be five years old is generally here to stay a while. Surprisingly, the years five to fourteen are the safest years a human being will ever know. On every continent, the overall death rate increases, frequently doubles, when one enters the fifteen to twenty-four age range — the age of entering the labor force for most young people, and the age of entering childbearing for females. Those golden years of childhood one hears about appear to be strictly confined to ages five to fourteen. Table 11 shows that the bulk of the world's population in this age group is to be found in Asia — which has a growing share of a growing number of children. Populations in Africa and Latin America are also growing. This suggests that from a global policy point of view less attention should go to the children and youth of North America and Europe, which have only twelve percent of the world's children and adolescents between them, and most to Asia, Africa, and Latin America, where the great bulk of the world's children are.

In terms of the world health problems, infants and children at every age are far more vulnerable to death from infective-parasitic, respiratory and digestive system diseases in Africa, Asia (saving Japan) and Latin America than in Europe.[9] (Japan is more like a European than a third world country in all its death rates.) There are several major reasons for these differences in death rates. One has to do with sanitation systems and supplies of pure water, and one has to do with nutrition levels. Infants are highly vulnerable both to the consequences of poor sanitation, and to the consequences of poor nutrition. The lucky four- to fifteen-year-olds are the survivors of the microbes and malnutrition of early childhood.

One very important right for children then is the right to pure water and a good community sanitation system. It is far more important for under-fives than for any other members of a community. A second and more difficult to enunciate right, is the right to adequate nutrition in the first five years of life. The adequacy of the nutritional level determines

Table 10. Death Rates per 100,000 Population by Causes of Death, 1972-73, Children and Young Adults

	Africa	Asia			Euro-North America						Latin America		
	Egypt	Japan	Philip-pines	Thailand	France	Hungary	Sweden	Spain	United Kingdom	United States	Colombia	Mexico	Peru
All Causes													
0	11156.6	1132.1	7007.6	2182.0	1262.5	3383.6	984.8	1520.6	1687.5	1847.0	5824.8	5185.3	7237.8
1 - 4	2473.6	98.5	949.3	468.8	74.5	84.5	42.3	90.9	69.0	80.9	748.1	723.7	744.1
5 - 14	184.5	35.4	157.5	159.6	36.3	34.2	28.4	38.8	30.5	40.8	129.3	125.6	93.0
15 - 24	241.3	82.2	163.5	235.1	106.9	83.3	72.8	75.1	69.4	127.7	187.8	213.4	133.3
25 - 34	238.2	105.1	232.6	311.2	115.8	130.5	91.6	106.5	79.5	153.9	254.2	345.3	196.2
Infective/Parasitic													
0	260.5	57.8	1431.0	302.2	86.7	135.7	15.5	204.5	66.4	60.4	1707.9	1547.3	2216.9
1 - 4	45.8	7.5	281.2	85.0	4.3	6.3	2.7	14.9	6.0	3.5	301.1	294.8	294.3
5 - 14	11.9	1.0	43.5	30.7	0.8	0.8	0.4	2.5	1.1	1.0	34.5	35.9	24.2
15 - 24	17.8	1.6	37.6	29.0	1.3	1.5	0.7	2.6	1.2	1.3	18.5	29.9	29.4
25 - 34	21.8	3.2	62.7	32.9	2.3	2.0	2.8	4.0	1.2	2.0	26.4	47.3	44.0
Respiratory System													
0	3161.1	135.9	2376.2	817.6	53.9	312.4	18.2	334.9	239.7	165.9	1432.7	1660.4	2893.5
1 - 4	1038.5	12.5	445.1	78.6	5.4	13.6	2.7	13.2	13.1	9.9	160.9	176.3	269.0
5 - 14	44.5	3.1	44.6	18.0	1.5	1.8	0.4	3.1	2.3	2.2	14.2	16.4	25.3
15 - 24	13.6	3.0	19.3	13.8	2.5	1.5	1.4	3.0	4.2	3.4	8.1	14.8	19.2
25 - 34	14.4	3.4	20.1	17.5	2.6	2.8	1.9	4.7	4.2	5.5	9.6	24.9	23.3
Digestive System													
0	5174.7	22.9	81.7	149.5	28.2	19.2	17.3	30.5	31.1	27.4	57.6	61.3	144.0
1 - 4	1201.7	1.4	14.0	7.4	1.0	3.1	--	2.3	1.2	1.5	7.6	12.4	13.5
5 - 14	24.9	0.8	5.9	3.9	0.9	0.8	--	1.6	0.6	0.6	3.3	3.8	2.7
15 - 24	22.2	1.9	9.1	8.0	1.7	2.0	1.1	2.3	1.4	1.7	5.6	9.2	7.8
25 - 34	28.4	4.9	16.2	16.1	6.7	4.6	4.4	6.3	2.7	7.8	10.4	28.1	14.1
Accidents & Violence													
0	21.0	61.3	74.6	18.5	102.5	42.9	15.5	35.9	50.2	62.9	47.6	58.7	41.1
1 - 4	42.5	43.9	24.2	24.0	27.4	25.3	10.8	19.9	17.8	34.8	33.3	44.6	23.5
5 - 14	36.5	15.6	17.4	19.3[d]	17.4[e]	13.1[f]	12.2[g]	12.6	11.4	22.4[c]	25.1[b]	26.7	13.0
15 - 24	72.6[a]	49.4	38.9	69.5[d]	77.2[e]	50.6[f]	51.8[g]	39.9	40.9	94.3[c]	86.4[b]	84.0	27.5
25 - 34	43.6	43.8	41.3	83.3[d]	64.8[e]	65.5[f]	51.6[g]	42.3	31.1	86.3[c]	99.1[b]	112.3	36.4

SOURCE: Table 7, "Deaths According to Cause by Sex and Age: Death Rates Specific for Sex and Age per 100,000 Population"(United Nations, 1976e).

Table 11. Population Movements in the Relative Share of the Continents in the World, Total for the 5-14 Year Age Group (Both Sexes) Between 1965 and 1980

	1965 (%)	1980 (%)	Diff.	
Africa	10.1	11.8	+1.7	Afrique
Northern America	5.7	4.4	-1.3	Amérique septentrionale
Latin America	8.3	9.5	+1.2	Amérique latine
Asia	59.7	61.8	+2.1	Asie
Europe	9.6	7.8	-1.8	Europe
Oceania	0.5	0.5	--	Océanie
U.S.S.R.	6.1	4.2	-1.9	U.R.S.S.
World	100.0	100.0	0.0	Monde

Source: United Nations (1975e:160).

the vulnerability to other diseases. Children rarely die of starvation, except in times of famine; they die because they have no bodily resistance to other diseases to which they are exposed. The actual food supply available to a family does not ensure that enough food will be available to under-fives. Food portions are traditionally distributed in such a way that the fathers, and all male children over five, are well supplied with food. Five to fourteeen year-old females are next in line in terms of adequacy of nutrition. Taboos about what girls and women should eat, whether prepregnant, pregnant or nursing, usually cut down on the available foods to women after puberty. As long as infants are breast fed, they are usually well fed, if the mother's food taboos are not too stringent, or if there is not a general food shortage. In any food shortage, women's food supplies are by custom cut down before men's. Also, male infants are better fed than female. Slightly older male children may share the breast with an infant sister and get the better part of a mother's milk. When pseudomodernizing practices of using the bottle have been introduced, babies are almost invariably undernourished. Bottle feeding introduces the twin hazard for babies of unsanitary preparation of the infant formula, and excessive dilution of the formula with water as an economy measure. As a result, infant morbidity rates shoot upwards. It has been estimated in Latin America that one half of all deaths to children under five are malnutrition related. The figures for Africa and South Asia would be higher still (Eckholm and Newland 1977:74).

Lack of knowledge of the nutritional needs of the infant leads to skimping on formula ingredients. The right to be breast fed is an important right of all babies, when this is medically possible for the mother, since it is a major guarantee of adequate nutrition for the first year of life. The right to adequate weaning foods and to a reasonable share of the family food supply from weaning to age of five is another important right, not acknowledged in many societies because there is little understanding of the food needs of the one to five-year old child. Equal rights to available food for girl and boy children is another important right. Additionally, proper understanding of and meeting of the food needs of the adolescent girl and pregnant and nursing mother, all of which statuses the teenage girl is likely to experience, is an important right. Girls may survive repeated pregnancies and nursings, but the babies they give birth to may be sickly. They will stay sickly through poor quality mother's milk or poorer bottle feeding, thus crippling later physical, intellectual and social development of pre-pubertal and adolescent youngsters. This crippling permanently limits adult capabilities (National Academy of Sciences 1973).

The difficulty of establishing minimum nutritional need levels for infants, children and adults in all societies has been repeatedly stated. Climate, type of diet, genetic equipment, size, activity, general health level, socio-emotional wellbeing and habituation all determine how much food an individual needs. It is also impossible to distribute food differentially to various parts of the population. Programs aimed at nutritional needs for school-age children are of limited use since this is a more adequately fed population, relatively speaking. Food sent home with school-age children will not necessarily be given to needy younger siblings. Increasing the total food supply available to the poorer families of every society, and establishing through every educational means available *the rights of infants to the breast and of pre-fives to a sufficient share of family food* is a basic need in many societies. The Indian saying, much used in nutrition programs, "Your Child's Plate is His Horoscope," needs to be extended so there will be a better realization of the lifetime consequences for children and women as well as of men, of the share of family food that goes on their plates. Food deprivation of small children is not necessarily due to food shortages, or to parental neglect, but to ignorance of food needs. The more children and women are redefined as persons, and not objects, the more quickly their right to food will be recognized.

Problems of malnutrition in the first world are very different from the problems of malnutrition in the third world. As the Worldwatch Publication, *The Two Faces of Malnutrition* (Eckholm and Record 1976) makes clear, for first world populations the problem is the wrong kinds of food,

Table 12. Death Rates per 100,000 Population by Accidents, Poisonings and Violence, 1972-73, for Children and Young Adults

	Africa	Asia			Euro-North America						Latin America		
	Egypt	Japan	Philippines	Thailand	France	Hungary	Sweden	Spain	United Kingdom	United States	Colombia	Mexico	Peru
All Accidents & Violence													
0	21.0	61.3	74.6	18.5	102.5	41.3	15.5	35.9	50.2	62.9	47.6	58.7	41.1
1 - 4	42.5	43.9	24.2	24.0	27.4	21.1	10.8	19.9	17.8	34.8	33.3	44.6	23.5
5 - 14	36.5	15.6	17.4	19.3	17.4	12.9	12.2	12.6	11.4	22.4	25.1	26.7	13.0
15 - 24	72.6	49.4	38.9	69.5	77.2	55.8	51.8	39.9	40.9	94.3	86.4	84.0	27.5
25 - 34	43.6	43.8	41.3	83.3	64.8	67.5	51.6	42.3	31.1	86.3	99.1	112.3	36.4
Motor Vehicles													
0	0.7	2.8	0.2	1.0	5.4	3.2	1.8	3.7	1.6	9.2	1.6	1.8	1.7
1 - 4	1.1	13.6	0.9	3.5	7.9	4.4	3.2	5.4	6.0	11.6	5.1	3.6	2.3
5 - 14	2.1	6.5	1.4	5.7	7.8	4.8	7.2	4.6	6.7	10.7	7.6	3.8	2.1
15 - 24	2.0	20.8	1.6	18.9	41.4	19.8	22.9	19.9	25.3	47.4	12.5	10.3	3.4
25 - 34	1.6	12.1	2.4	20.8	25.7	18.3	11.5	20.1	12.1	30.3	13.9	12.4	8.2
Other Transportation													
0	—	0.4	—	0.3	0.5	—	—	0.1	0.1	0.1	0.4	0.2	0.2
1 - 4	0.3	2.0	0.0	0.2	0.1	0.3	0.2	0.3	0.2	0.3	0.2	0.0	0.1
5 - 14	0.5	1.2	0.0	0.2	0.5	1.2	0.7	0.3	0.3	0.8	0.3	0.1	—
15 - 24	1.3	1.2	0.2	0.8	0.9	3.9	2.3	1.2	1.3	2.3	1.1	0.2	0.1
25 - 34	1.0	1.4	0.3	1.2	1.3	3.0	2.1	1.6	1.6	3.3	1.6	0.6	0.4
Fires													
0	4.0	2.8	0.7	2.3	2.1	1.1	0.9	2.1	3.6	4.6	6.3	4.8	7.5
1 - 4	12.5	1.8	0.2	1.1	2.8	1.5	1.1	1.7	2.6	5.1	5.6	5.1	3.3
5 - 14	6.3	0.6	0.1	0.3	0.7	0.1	0.4	0.1	0.5	1.6	1.4	1.3	0.7
15 - 24	23.3	0.7	0.0	0.3	0.7	0.3	0.3	0.5	0.6	1.2	1.3	1.6	0.8
25 - 34	8.7	0.8	0.0	0.4	0.8	0.5	0.5	0.4	0.8	1.7	1.2	2.5	1.1
Drowning													
0	—	4.7	2.5	4.1	0.8	0.5	—	1.2	0.6	1.8	3.5	1.7	1.7
1 - 4	—	15.6	5.2	14.8	4.4	2.9	2.3	4.0	2.4	5.7	9.1	4.9	5.9
5 - 14	—	3.6	3.5	6.6	2.2	2.4	1.5	2.6	1.5	3.4	4.4	2.8	2.3
15 - 24	—	2.4	2.6	4.4	3.4	2.9	2.0	3.9	1.4	5.0	8.2	6.2	4.5
25 - 34	—	1.4	1.6	3.6	2.1	1.0	2.1	2.4	0.7	2.1	5.8	4.2	3.6

Table 12 (cont'd)

	Africa	Asia			Euro-North America						Latin America		
	Egypt	Japan	Philip-pines	Thailand	France	Hungary	Sweden	Spain	United Kingdom	United States	Colombia	Mexico	Peru
Industrial Accidents													
0	0.3	1.4	0.9	0.6	0.4	1.1	--	0.4	1.2	0.9	1.2	0.3	0.7
1 – 4	0.7	3.2	0.9	0.6	0.8	5.8	0.2	0.9	1.0	1.8	1.0	0.5	0.3
5 – 14	0.9	0.7	1.4	0.6	0.4	1.0	0.5	0.5	0.5	0.9	1.1	0.6	0.4
15 – 24	2.5	2.2	2.2	2.7	1.3	2.7	1.9	2.0	1.4	2.7	2.4	1.8	0.7
25 – 34	1.2	3.4	2.7	2.5	1.6	3.3	1.9	2.2	1.6	3.4	3.0	1.8	1.5
All Other Accidents													
0	15.4	36.5	63.1	7.6	87.6	23.1	11.9	23.9	32.0	33.5	18.8	36.0	22.7
1 – 4	25.5	2.4	11.5	1.9	7.6	2.0	1.8	3.8	2.0	3.4	4.8	16.1	6.5
5 – 14	25.6	0.6	6.3	2.9	3.5	0.7	0.6	2.6	0.5	1.4	3.9	8.0	5.1
15 – 24	40.6	0.8	10.3	9.4	15.2	0.9	0.8	6.3	1.2	2.2	6.8	17.3	7.5
25 – 34	29.6	0.8	13.1	11.3	13.1	2.1	0.9	7.6	1.2	2.7	8.2	23.7	11.4
Suicides													
0	--	--	--	--	--	--	--	--	--	--	--	--	--
1 – 4	--	--	--	--	--	--	--	--	--	--	--	--	--
5 – 14	--	0.6	0.1	0.5	0.3	1.0	0.4	0.2	0.1	0.3	0.4	--	--
15 – 24	--	16.5	3.3	10.5	7.7	20.3	15.0	1.4	4.4	10.2	7.6	1.3	3.5
25 – 34	--	18.0	2.0	6.3	12.1	32.2	20.5	2.7	7.2	14.7	6.2	1.2	2.7
Homicides													
0	--	7.9	0.5	0.5	1.5	11.3	--	0.3	5.9	5.3	2.9	1.4	2.0
1 – 4	--	2.3	0.1	0.6	0.4	0.5	1.1	0.0	1.1	1.8	0.4	0.7	0.7
5 – 14	--	0.8	0.2	1.4	0.1	0.3	0.4	--	0.4	0.9	1.1	1.0	0.2
15 – 24	--	0.8	3.5	20.2	0.6	1.7	0.9	0.1	1.3	13.5	27.1	16.9	1.2
25 – 34	--	1.4	4.3	35.3	1.4	2.0	1.2	0.5	1.2	18.5	39.9	31.1	1.3
War													
0	--	--	0.2	--	--	--	--	--	--	--	0.1	--	--
1 – 4	--	--	--	--	--	--	--	--	--	--	--	--	--
5 – 14	--	--	0.0	--	--	--	--	--	--	--	--	0.0	--
15 – 24	--	--	0.3	--	--	--	--	--	--	0.1	0.1	--	--
25 – 34	--	--	0.4	--	--	--	--	--	--	--	--	--	--

SOURCE: Table 7, "Deaths According to Cause by Sex and Age: Death Rates Specific for Sex and Age per 100,000 Population" (United Nations, 1976e).

not insufficient amounts. Many factors contribute to this problem. There are food packaging and preservation practices, the premium placed on "fast foods" by busy parents and the taste for sweet and over-processed foods fostered in children by TV advertising, and implemented by fast food slot machines available to children in schools and neighborhoods. There is the decline in the practice of children packing their own lunches under parental eyes in the family kitchen in the mornings, and a general decline in the amount of food preparation that takes place in family kitchens. At the same time there is widespread overconsumption of animal fats, and overeating in general. What is being increasingly reported in the United States press is a decline in the practice of nutritional knowledge once widely taught in the home, the community and the schools.[10] For children this often means few good meals in a week and less than optimal health. The effects for children are beginning to show up in an appearance of signs of arteriosclerosis in teenagers, formerly only a disease of the middle aged. Hypertension is also increasingly appearing among the young, and it is estimated that ten to twenty percent of all United States children are overweight. Vulnerability to the later appearance of bowel and esophageal cancer, due to a combination of the effects of food additives, alcohol and tobacco is also rising (Eckholm and Record 1976:32-46).

The rise in overall death rates after age fifteen is not due to a sudden increase in mortality from the three categories of diseases in Table 9, or others not mentioned there. They are rather due to the increase in deaths from the fourth category, Accidents and Violence. The death rate from these causes triples or quadruples between the five to fourteen age group, and the fifteen to twenty-four age group. In order to interpret these figures better, Table 12 gives a breakdown of the types of causes of death by accidents and violence first presented in Table 10. Whereas for the previously discussed causes of death the third world children were the most vulnerable, now it is the first world youth rather than the third world youth who are particularly vulnerable to certain accident-related causes of death. Cars are the worst killers in Europe, North America and Japan. Industrial accidents, interestingly, are equally dangerous for countries in all stages of industrialization.[11] Death by suicide for young people is high on every continent, reflecting perhaps the despair that teenagers feel in facing a difficult, rapidly changing world with so little status, freedom and resources to solve their own problems. Deaths by homicide are high in some countries, low in others, without regard to level of industrialization. United States deaths by homicide for fifteen to twenty-four year olds is higher than for any European countries. For under-fives, cars, fire and drowning are dangerous on every continent.

Surprisingly, industrial accidents are a first world danger to under fives.

If ever there was a case for "protection" of children, it would be from public hazards such as cars and industrial accidents. Yet death rates are high in every age group. Who is to do the protecting? What kind of right is involved?

CHILDREN AS VICTIMS OF EDUCATIONAL SYSTEMS

Pride in the quality of education available to children in the "old industrialized" societies and concern to extend that quality of education to children in third world countries has characterized the major drives by UNESCO and third world countries to make schooling available to all children, at least through the primary level. A combination of falling death rates and rapid population increases, along with natural catastrophes and productivity failures in both the agricultural and industrial sectors has led to negative economic growth rates in some third world countries and placed them far behind in their own schedule of making eduction available to children. In the first world the problems are different. With school dropout rates[12] and teenage suicide and alcoholic and drug addiction rates rising in a number of countries, questions about the quality and relevance of classroom education as it has developed in this century in the West are being raised. In the mid-1970s for the first time serious questions are being raised about the effect of existing educational practices and future educational plans on national well being both in the more and the less industrialized countries. The latest UNESCO report on youth reports growing awareness in the third world that education not only perpetuates but aggravates existing social and economic inequality, and does so from elementary school on because the difference in quality of schooling available to the better off and to the masses. This in turn limits the opportunity of low and modest income people for higher education and closes off employment alternatives. Rigid hierarchial educational structures are also beginning to be seen as an obstacle to equal learning opportunities, on all continents. The protest against the sharpening of the division between intellectual and physical labor that comes with industrialization and is felt early in the school system, is also being heard on all continents. Cuba, China and Guinea Bissau are cited by UNESCO as engaging in significant educational experiments to overcome the above problems (United Nations 1977b).

Table 13 documents the existing aspiration level for universal education in third world countries, comparable to that in Europe and North America (first two rows), and indicates the gap between aspiration and reality for Level one and Level two enrollments. Generally Level one, primary education, covers six to eight years, and Level two, secondary education, covers four to six years, making a desired total of twelve years according to educational planning. Few third world countries have been able to go beyond a theoretical six years of compulsory schooling. The reality in these countries, even for children actually enrolled, is that few complete six years during the age period allotted to primary education. The dropout rate may be as high as eighty percent or more in the primary years. On the other hand young people may acquire the education in later years, either by returning to school or through nonformal education programs, so the completion rate for elementary schooling may be sixty percent where it has appeared to be twenty percent.[13] Increasingly programs for older children, youth and adults are being provided in which rapid functional education and training can take place. In the future, the innovations being tried for older children and adults may filter down to younger children. For the time being, however, most elementary age children, if they are in school at all, are pursuing a formalistic learning which does little to facilitate problem solving in their real life situations and renders their literacy skills inert through lack of interest and use. UNICEF is making serious efforts to change this at the elementary level, particularly in a program to "ruralize" classroom education in rural areas. It has also experiemented with various approaches to nonformal education. UNICEF's New Paths to Learning study uncovered one major source of resistance to educational reform: "the unwillingness of parents and pupils to accept alternatives to formal eduation" (United

Table 13. Legal Provisions of Education and School Enrollments

	Africa			Asia		
	Algeria	Egypt	Tanzania	Japan	Philip-pines	Thailand
Ages for Compulsory School[b]	6-14	6-12	--	6-15	7-12	7-14
# Years of Compulsory School[b]	8	6	--	9	6	7
% School-Age Children Enrolled in Level 1[a]	70	70	38	98	112	81
% School-Age Children Enrolled in Level 2[a]	9	30	2	86	42	13
Number of Human Rights Treaties Ratified, Dec. 1973[c]	8	7	--	2	8	1

[a]Boulding Global Data Bank, n.d.

[b]Table 3, "Educational Structures and Enrollment Ratios by Country (United Nations, 1975d).

Nations 1977b:21). The inappropriate role models of western schooling will not easily be cast aside.

It has been known for some time that certain proportions of vocational to general education for school-age children make a great deal of difference in a country's economic growth (Bennett 1967), and that literacy skills alone do not necessarily produce problem solving competence (Schuman, Inkeles and Smith 1967). While there is increasing talk about the need for vocational education, it is not a well developed part of many third world educational programs, particularly at the primary school level which provides the only opportunity many children will ever have to gain vocational type skills. Even when vocational training opportunities do exist, they may be too long in duration and not well synchronized with actual employment opportunities; high dropout rates and poor placement records for graduates have given vocational training a bad name in various areas. (Note the discussion on vocational training in *Children and Youth in National Development in Latin America* United Nations 1966a.) More recent attempts at developing, or redeveloping, apprenticeship programs that provide on-the-job training hold some promise for furture cohorts of young people (United Nations 1972b:45; Gillette 1974:26-27).

The problems of faulty educational planning and inadequate and excessively compartmentalized literacy training is not an exclusively third world problem. Many children with only four years of formal schooling, whether they live in Upper Volta or the United States, cannot read by the

Table 13 (cont'd)

Europe and North America						Latin America		
France	Hungary	Sweden	Spain	United Kingdom	United States	Colombia	Mexico	Peru
6–16	6–16	7–16	6–13	5–16	6, 7– 16, 18	7–12	6–14	6–15
9	10	9	8	11	12	5	6	9
124	102	94	77	111	102	95	105	109
66	31	94	38	72	100	24	20	36
11	9	15	5	12	4	5	5	3

[c]The maximum number of treaties that could be ratified is 18.

time they are adults if they do not continue to use their literacy skills. The high estimates of functional illiteracy in the United States for these reasons of nonuse (one 1975 estimate was twenty-three million adults) are not encouraging to those who focus only on establishing a minimum number of years for children in the classroom ("Twenty-three Million Adults" 1975).

Children have a right to have book learning relate to the world they must deal with, and they have a right to realistic presentations in their textbooks of the range of possible roles open to them. Third world children may be exposed to material appropriate for European children only. (Our own five children, studying in Jamaican elementary schools in 1960, had geography textbooks about "our fisherman in the North Sea." and botany texts with drawings of the primrose, a flower that never could grow in Jamaica.) First world children may come to know less and less about the communities they live in. It has been well documented that American children are reading less and less, and have increasingly limited vocabularies. Girls and boys in both first and third world countries are confronted with severe sex stereotyping in their elementary textbooks. Minority children in every country face similar problems of stereotyping. The drive to "clean up" textbooks with regard to all kinds of ethnic and sex stereotyping has been gaining momentum in the last decade. Cutting across the increasing sterility of some classroom learning are the new developments in community based learning, community apprenticeships, and a variety of common sense efforts to bring children back into the real world they must share with adults. The efforts are too few, and one hopes they are not too late.

HUMAN RIGHTS OF CHILDREN AND YOUTH: WELFARE PROVISIONS, AND LEGAL STATUS

Welfare provisions are never made directly to children, but only to parents or legally responsible adults. Operative family allowance provisions that guarantee support of the state for children exist in few countries. Of the fifteen we have been studying in this paper, only four have family allowance provisions: France, Hungary, Sweden and the United Kingdom. In Hungary and the United Kingdom, it is estimated that only fifty percent of the children eligible are covered (Iyer 1966:484-85). (In many parts of the third world, because of the extended family system, children are "covered" through the mutual aid system of the extended family, and the presence or absence of state welfare provisions is no guide to an understanding of the actual care provided.)

The last row in Table 13 shows the level of commitment to United Nations human rights treaties by these fifteen countries. Eighteen is the maximum number of treaties that could be ratified. The mean number ratified is eight, less than half. Varying combinations of poverty, lack of conviction about the importance of human rights rhetoric and its legal ratification, and lack of interest in human rights as a concept, contribute to this sorry picture. Commitment to the provision of economic and social services specifically for children will under these conditions be minimal. The United Nations pamphlet on *Family, Child and Youth Welfare Services in Africa* has some very realistic points to make on this general subject, both with regard to family service and to education (United Nations 1966c).

The fact that welfare is not provided directly to children leaves those who are living in seriously inadequate and possibly poverty-ridden homes, and those who have been expelled from their homes, very vulnerable to abuse and delinquency. If they do earn money, it may be taken from them by adults in the household without proper provision being made for their own needs. If they do not earn money, they may be pushed or pulled into theft and violence. There is a very widespread conviction in nearly all societies that children should not be held "responsible" for criminal acts in the same way adults are responsible, so provision for special treatment of juvenile offenders is nearly universal. The age below which children are considered incapable of crime varies from country to country. In Scotland it is still eight years of age, though ten or twelve is more commonly established as the age below which children are "incapable of guile." Ten to fourteen year old offenders have special legal protection in most countries, and fourteen to eighteen year olds go before juvenile courts. In some countries youth have some special treatment as young adult offenders from eighteen to twenty-five or as old as thirty, before they become "regular"adult offenders.

The social *intention* to protect children from exposure to hardened criminals and the opportunity to be socialized into a life of crime is more or less seriously sabotaged in most countries by the emergent reality of the special institutions — borstals, juvenile detention centers, training centers — devised for the protection of children. These instituions sometimes socialize youth more effectively into crime than adult prisons could do. The problems cut across political ideologies and types of economic systems, so that socialist countries share with capitalist countries the challenge of adequate response to "young offenders." The very screening of children from regular trial procedure may render them more vulnerable than adults to false charges — charges which may never be disproved — as has been documented in various studies.[15] One of the main stimuli to the children's rights movement in the United States was the famous Gault case, in which a fifteen year old boy was in effect kept imprisoned for two years because of a joking phone call to a neighbor who had no sense of humor and had him picked up by the police. He was handled in juvenile court proceedings which denied him due process (In re Gault 387 US 1, 1967).

The fact documented extensively in the records of court proceeding on behalf of children against their parents, that some families are not good for their children, that they may prevent them from receiving economic aid, welfare services, and health and educational opportunities that children are entitled to by law, and that they may further abuse and neglect them and contribute to their delinquent behavior, suggests that there needs to be continual rethinking of legislation on the subject of child welfare.[16] Court procedures for intervention "in the best interests" of the child are far from satisfactory. "The best interests" standard, initially followed in most state interventions and explicitly used as the standard for adjudicating children's interests in proceedings evaluating parental care, is not properly a standard. Instead, it is a rationalization by decision-makers justifying their judgements about a child's future, like an empty vessel into which adult perceptions and prejudices are poured. It does not offer guidelines for how adult powers should be exercised. Seductively, it implies that there is a best alternative for children deprived of their family. Often there is no "best alternative." It would however be appropriate to make careful provision for children to seek a guardian as an alternative to inadequate parents if they are too young to live alone, and for children to be legally emancipated if they have demonstrated the capacity to live independently and be self-supporting.

It is easy to make the horrified response: What, let children change families at their own whim? Or: How can anyone judge whether a young person has demonstrated the capacity to live independently and be self-supporting? At the least, mechanisms at the community level ought to exist by means of which young persons can raise such questions without fear of reprisal. As one eighty-three year old volunteer worker with children commented, "You are fighting deep-rooted prejudices against 'naughty children.' " It is hard for a "troublesome child" to be taken seriously, yet running away from a punishing home situation may "be a healthy reaction to an impossible situation" (Wakin 1975:18, 128). The very fact that teenage young people in fairly large numbers seem to be unable to protect themselves from physical abuse at home, as pointed out in the discussion of child abuse, raises the question as to how well they will be able to handle themselves outside the home. Clearly they need help. But so do abused adults. Physical abuse of teenagers comes perhaps closer to the category of spouse abuse, and the same kinds of facilities increasingly becoming available to women who cannot protect themselves against abusing husbands ought to be available to teenagers. Now that reports of husband abuse are also coming to the attention of agencies, it seems logical to plan community facilities that are avilable for teenagers and adults of both sexes who need it.

I do not know of any country where there is any body or case of statutory law setting forth the rights of children. 1967 is the first year in which a court of the United States ruled on the constitutional rights of a child (Gault 387 US 1, 1967), and then the court ruled on procedural matters only. There is no legal agreement on "who is a child." In the United States a thirteen-year old can be tried for and convicted of murder, but an eighteen year old needs parental consent to marry and an under twenty-one cannot sign contracts, sell property or do any other business that will be upheld in a court of law, even if that person is married and supporting children.[18] Adolescents are also denied service on juries, elected or appointed political office, control of property and person, and a host of other participatory rights and decision-making powers (Forer 1973:29). Children do not have the right to choose their own school, their own religion,[19] or the parent they would like to live with if their parents divorce. They do not have the right of privacy over parental censorship, nor the right to the money they earn, until they are twenty-one. The fact that eighteen-year olds have made so little use of their right to vote may partly be due to the fact that freedom has little meaning in the context of a general lack of personal autonomy.

While in most countries twenty-one is still the age of majority for young persons, a number of countries are now lowering the age to twenty or eighteen. Table 14 provides current data on the age of majority around the world. Things are improving for young people, but slowly.

Whenever a minor comes into the courts in a suit against parents, as happens more often than one might suspect, the court decision is nearly always weighted in favor of the "sanctity of the home," meaning that it is better to leave the child or young person subject to parents no matter how bad, than to break up a home. It is this same sanctity of the home concept that underlies the United Nations Declaration of the Rights of the Child. Katz, Schroeder and Sidman (1973) amply document the injustices to children and young people that this judicial attitude produces. The technical concept of emancipation, a basic tenet of family law in a number of countries, has begun in this century to be conceived as a device for "releasing children from their filial ties where circumstances so warranted." Judicial emancipation, "refers to the termination of certain rights and obligations attaching to the parent-child relationship dur-

Table 14. Age of Majority

	21 years	20 years	19 years	18 years[1]
Europe	Belgium Italy Monaco Netherlands	Denmark Finland Norway Sweden		Bulgaria Hungary Romania Czechoslovakia USSR Yugoslavia
North America	United States (with four exceptions)	United States (State of Hawaii)	United States (State of Alaska)	United States[2] (States of Kentucky and Georgia)
Latin America and the Caribbean	Chile Costa Rica Guyana Jamaica Trinidad and Tobago			
Asia and the Pacific	Australia India New Zealand Singapore	Japan		Laos Pakistan[3] Turkey
Africa	Algeria Ivory Coast Ghana Mauritius Liberia[4] Arab Republic of Egypt Sierra Leone			

[1]Although the legislation of the United Kingdom has not been examined in this survey, it should be pointed out that the age of majority there was lowered to eighteen in 1970 (Family Law Reform, 1969).

[2]In eleven other states, girls come of age at eighteen.

[3]In reply to the Unesco questionnaire, the Minister of Education of Pakistan stated that the age of civil majority is eighteen for boys and sixteen for girls. However, even after attaining their majority, young people have no responsibilities until they begin to earn their living independently.

[4]The reply to the Unesco questionnaire from the Bureau of Youth of Liberia states that the age of maturity is twenty-one for boys and eighteen for girls.

ing the child's minority" (1973:213-214). It confers on minors either the full rights of civil majority or more limited rights regarding administration of property. The minimum age for emancipation varies from thirteen to eighteen. Usually the application for emancipation must be lodged by the parents and therefore cannot be done without their consent. If the emancipation is partial, parents are left with some responsibility for child support. If it is complete, all financial obligations between parties are severed. In the absence of legal emancipation, parents may demand their children's services in the home, and the wages they can earn outside it, with perfect legality until the young person is twenty-one.

A few countries, including the United States, are moving toward a general principle of statutory emancipation for "relief from the disabilities of a minor," *on request from the minor.* This makes the minor a full adult in the eyes of the law. Few cases have been allowed for young persons under eighteen, but there is one case in the United States of a thirteen-year old girl being emancipated. Persons concerned with the rights of children and youth are beginning to propose legal emancipation on request, at any age at which the individual is competent to go through the processes of applying for it, as a general human right. Legal and cultural traditions in most countries will be strongly opposed to this, and such a development is not likely to take place for a very long time. Since the age at which young people undertake autonomous business affairs varies greatly both within and between countries, it makes little sense to try to arrive at the proper age of legal emancipation. To have it available on request before age eighteen, and automatically at age eighteen, might best serve the diverse needs of the world's youth at this time.

This discussion has focused entirely on young people who are prepared to make their own life decisions and who may be seriously hampered by their families in doing this. Such circumstances may appear to be exceptional in any particular society, but it does not undermine sound social institutions to provide for individual disadvantage and suffering. A different but also important use of the principal of emancipation is to free an infant from parents unable or unwilling to care for it properly. Here the issue is more directly "protection," and making the infant free for adoption by others who can provide the nurturant setting all infants need. Similarly, emancipation for the purposes of establishing court-supervised guardianship for children too young to live alone but needing to be freed from an abusing family, can be an important use of the legal device. In this latter case the device is in danger of being misused, since children old enough to speak for themselves may not be adequately consulted in the choice of a guardian. Eternal vigilance against the dangers of protectionism is required.

The first longitudinal study ever made of children in foster care has recently been completed in the United States. Six hundred and twenty-four children were followed over a five year period. The findings go contrary to beliefs that foster care (as compared to parental care) is damaging to children, demostrating rather a clear picture of solid emotional and intellectual development of the "hard cases"—the children who were left in foster care continually for five years. The foster care option, the authors of this study point out, is worthy of continued serious consideration (Fanshel and Shinn 1978). What both foster care advocates, and advocates of "home care no matter how bad" agree on is that either of these arrangements is preferable to institutional care for children. Institutions do not, usually cannot, provide enough individuated care to children to ensure normal healthy development.

A broader question relates to the unavailability of adequate numbers of foster homes, and of the possibility of local, community based care for children and youth. There is no substitute for neighborhood awareness, and community participation, in providing a supportive environment for children and youth. As a recent Rockefeller Report (1977) points out, the "natural helpers" of the child are in the child's local community.

In Part II we have reviewed the victimage of children and youth in home, school, employment, welfare and legal settings. Comparing the materials presented here with the earlier materials on the participation of children and youth in society, it is clear that major imbalances and injustices exist with regard to what is expected of a young person in terms of responsibilities, and what is accorded to the young person in terms of rights. The concept of protection, while well-intentioned, often does not deal with the issues that arise. It appears that children and youth, like other minorities, should be treated as individuals and not subsumed under the category, family member protected by head-of-household. The emancipation of women from that category, is still in process, and few see even the need for a similar emancipation for children.

The proposed Declaration of Human Rights to Be Extended to Persons Under Twenty-One that follows is based on a distillation of the harmful constraints placed on young persons. Each constraint has been turned into its counterpart enablement. It will be for many a radical statement, but it speaks directly to the issues raised in this study and is based on systematically acquired knowledge about the capacities and activities of children and youth. As a set of principles concerning the participation of under twenty-ones in the difficult social tasks that lie before us, I believe it is worth serious consideration.

They are offered for purposes of public debate and reflection on the situation of children and youth in contemporary society, not as a set of principles to be adopted and implemented as they stand. I recognize that in society as it now exists, in most parts of the world, few of the principles could be easily implemented. In the industrialized world children and youth have been so overprotected that many could not respond creatively to the opportunities the principles represent. Neither could they cope with the withdrawal of protection implied in the right-to-work principle, since adults are so accustomed to exploiting children. In other world regions some of the rights enunciated are not yet recognized for adults and so can hardly be accepted as extending to children. The sad truth is that there is not enough human nurturance to go round for either the world's children or the world's adults, nor are adequate material resources available for two-thirds of the world's population. Yet by affirming the human potential in children, and envisioning an ideal, we make it possible to redirect social effort toward realizing such an ideal in the future. No society can create anything better than what it creates for its children.

Following the proposed Declaration of Rights we will turn to a review of current international planning for the future, particularly in the context of the second Decade of Development, with emphasis on the posibilities for involvment of children and youth in planning and action during this and following decades.

DECLARATION OF HUMAN RIGHTS TO BE EXTENDED TO PERSONS UNDER TWENTY-ONE

Children should be granted indivdual freedom and autonomy commensurate with their maturation and development and the burden should be upon those who abridge such freedom to show that such abridgement is necessary and actually in the young person's best interest.

Principle I
The right of personhood

The right to be regarded as a person within the family, at school, in the community and before the law. The right to a name and a nationality.

Principle II
The right to shelter, love and nurturance

The right to shelter, love and nurturance from infancy in a setting of mutually shared responsibility where skills of adulthood can be learned.

Principle III
The right to choice of domicile

The right to live away from home, to choose or make one's home when financially independent. The right to participate in choice of residence patterns if parents divorce. For the very young: the right to a court-appointed guardian if the family situation becomes abusive, the guardian to arrange and supervise acceptable alternative livings arrangements. The guardianship is to be reconsidered on request of the child.

Principle IV
The right to food and health

The right to adequate nutrition, safe water and adequate medical services. The right to seek and receive medical care on one's own initiative, and to choose the form of treatment when informed initiative is evident.

Principle V
The right to education

The right to education and training of one's choice, regardless of gender, racial or ethnic background, religion of parents, and the right of full access to the cultural heritage of one's choice in the pursuit of that education.

Principle VI
The right to work

The right to work and retain one's earnings at any age. The right to union participation and protection where unions exist, and the right to equal pay for equal work.

Principle VII
The right to equal treatment before the law

The right to enter into contractual relations, and to barter, buy and sell services and property, at any age when competence to define, agree to and carry out contracts is demonstrated through performance. Any legal disability placed on a child must be convincingly shown to be necessary and protective of the child's best interests.

The right to the same legal protections and guarantees in court that are available to persons over twenty-one.

Principle VIII
The right to voluntary parenthood

a. The right to contraceptive information and assistance for any young person of any age on request. The right to abortion on request for any young female of any age. The right of protection against rape, and assistance in case of rape, for any female from infancy on.

b. Full rights and responsibilities of legal parenthood for any young female of any age and marital status who has given birth to a child, with rights to whatever types of aid she requests.

c. Full rights of shared legal parenthood for a young male of any age and marital status who is acknowledged as father by mother of the child, who is invited by her to share responsibility, and who agrees to take responsibility. No unwed father may have rights of legal parenthood without the consent of the mother.

Principle IX
The right to peace and freedom

The right to live in peace, with political and religious freedom of belief; the right of full membership in and responsibility for the community of nations, and the right to travel freely everywhere. The right to refuse national military service and to choose alternative service of a socially constructive nature in its place, either at home or abroad.

CHILDREN AND YOUTH AND THE SECOND DEVELOPMENT DECADE

In this concluding section we will examine children and youth-related planning for the second development decade in the context of what has been presented about the actual contributions of these age groups to the general social welfare, and about the constraints, limitations and actual abuse they suffer because of their legal minority status.

The United Nations Children's Fund (UNICEF) report from 1976 focuses, understandably and properly, on children in developing countries, and points out that "the situation of children in many parts of the developing world had deteriorated further in 1975. The number of children dying from preventable diseases, suffering from severe malnutrition and missing the educational preparation for a decent life was clearly on the increase." At the same time, "Many governments had been forced to delay the implementation of development plans, or to shift resources within plans from social services to financially productive activities, thus seriously hampering the expansion of services for children" (United Nations 1976c:2). Not only have rising construction costs led to abandonment of service related building projects, but rising costs of training and education and of foods, medicines and transport, has led to a cutback or abandonment of many services that had been earlier instituted. "The 'quiet emergency' facing millions of children daily, to which UNICEF had been calling attention for many years, still existed" (United Nations 1976c:3).

UNICEF's focus has been on children under twelve and expectant and nursing mothers—an estimated total of nine million persons in urgent need in the third world. Any age cutoff is necessarily arbitrary, and among these under-twelves are many who are in the labor force and who are themselves providing a range of sevices to their families and communities. Thousands of smaller children, for example, are cared for by siblings aged eight to twelve (Stein 1965:66). The major thrust of UNICEF at present is to identify strategies and resources to expand

"Basic Services" for children and mothers. Since we know that many of these mothers are themselves teenagers, the Basic Services approach covers a wider range than first appears. Taken in itself, the Basic Services concept is a good one: to develop "a group of of mutually interacting Basic Services in the fields of maternal and child health, including family planning, nutrition, water supply, basic education, and supporting services for women" (United Nations 1976c:6). They are to be community based, labor intensive, using people with paraprofessional training who are themselves villagers, thereby mobilizing "that large proportion of the population in many countries that constituted an untapped reservoir of energy, potential skill and leadership, namely, women" (United Nations 1976c:6).[21]

Given the mandate with which UNICEF was started, these are appropriate goals as far as they go and in fact UNICEF has done extraordinary things with extremely limited resources in its brief decades of existence. It is to be hoped that the concerted attention of the approximately twenty United Nations agencies that are collaborating with UNICEF to make the International Year of the Child an occasion for giving a major new thrust to development programs as they relate to children, women and families, will indeed succeed in this goal. However, as long as the actual econmic production activities of children and teenaged parents and youth, and the level of family and community responsibility that very young persons exercise, are not taken account of, the program will fall short of what it could be. If the agencies focus primarily on concepts of protection and service, underplaying autonomy and self-help, they will fail to connect with their most vital allies. So far I have not seen any reference in all the United Nations documentation on the International Year of the Child to consulting with or working with children, or even to consulting youth about children. The theme is only, what can be done *for* the child in this Year.

UNICEF and other agencies concerned to help children, youth and mothers leave untapped many of the very resources referred to in the quotation earlier. In the long run training villagers as paraprofessionals may indeed increase the self-help potentials of a community, but very often the outcome is a new local elite replicating attitudes of urban-trained professionals. This has been the sad outcome in regard to the role and status of teachers of village schools, in all too many cases. An additional problem with the mothers and children approach is that it reenforces social attitudes that leave all child care responsiblities to mothers and their older children, and does not create the conditions under which fathers are brought more fully into the parenting process. Implementing a program for women which promotes their labor force participation during the second development decade while reenforcing their primary responsibility for child care will in the long run create the same kinds of problems that first world countries are experiencing as women move into the labor force in greater numbers under urban, industrial conditions. There is less and less parenting of children because of the work load of mothers, and children fall between the cracks—not given responsibility or meaningful community roles, left "to play" with a lack of appropriate settings or caring adults to interact with. Community child care facilties never develop at the rate community planners intend, in countries at any level of wealth, including the United States.

Efforts of national governments to increase coordination among different child-serving ministries in the national planning process, and the United Nations' goal of increasing inadequate budgets to fund more Basic Services, are important steps and should by no means be undervalued. Neither should the emphasis on community development, paraprofessional training and community self-help. However, just as earlier development programs have failed because of lack of recognition of the actual economic and social roles of women which were either ignored or actually undercut by assistance programs, so present development programs will fail because of the lack of recognition of the actual economic and social roles of children. Money aimed at increasing the quality of child care, will be money largely wasted if it is directed to a kind of "protection" that is irrelevant to the actual situation of children.

In this study it has been repeatedly emphasized that there is no automatic cutoff point below which children are children, and above which they are adult. The legal definition of minority, which lumps all persons together under the age of twenty-one is clearly nonsense. But only by continuously working at a more accurate understanding and description of what persons of different ages actually do, ignoring categories as far as possible of "under twelves" and "twelve to fifteen" and "sixteen to twenty," will planners be able to facilitate the release of the full development potential of any society. Since the only persons who know what individuals at these various age do are the persons of those ages themselves—adults' powers of observation having been seriously weakened by too-long residence in the sealed off world of development bureaucracy—one important way that societal potential can actually be released is through the participation of young persons of various ages in the planning process. This is equally true at the village level, at the level of national planning, and for international endeavors.

The interaction of many ages in the planning process will seem unthinkable to professionals accustomed to working with like-minded colleagues. What could children and young persons know that would be relevant? Yet the insight that there are things that youth know that adults do not is beginning to appear in planning literature. Published preceedings of the Round Table Conference on "Planning for the Needs of Children in Developing Countries" (Stein 1965) contains several references to the need to understand the actual situation of children and to draw on the views of youth in planning. Statements by Mr. Ahmed Ben Salah of Tunisia and Professor Eugen Pusic of Yugoslavia on involvement of representatives of organized youth groups in national planning were noteworthy on this regard (Stein 1965:75-77). The involvement of representatives of organized youth groups is obviously the easiest way to begin, and the Summary of Recommendations from the Symposium on the Participation of Youth in the Second United Nations Development Decade are very specific on how this can be done. The following sixteen points are taken from a slightly longer list:

1. Popular participation should be an integral part of the philosophy and practice of development which contributes to the benefit both of society and of the individual person. Participation should cover all areas of development and all phases of decision-making, implementation and evaluation;
2. Participation by youth should be seen and practised by governments and by the international community as part of popular participation as a whole;
3. There should be clear recognition of the fact that in many parts of the world popular participation, including that of youth, is impeded by existing political, economic and social systems; it should also be recognized that popular participation itself is necessary in order to bring about changes in these systems;
4. Youth's struggle for national liberation should be supported in all ways possible: this struggle should be seen as a means of implementing the United Nations Charter and the Declaration of Human Rights and as a prerequisite to the acheivement of development and youth participation in development.
5. The right and ability of every young man and woman to participate in development should be recognized and facilitated. This can be done only if it is accompanied by a process of their becoming aware of the realities of their situation, thus leading them to critical involvement in action;
6. Those in authority, whether in government, in education or in private life, should face the protest of youth as a form of critical evaluation rather than simply as a refusal to participate;
7. The right of youth to health, education and work should be

recognized as the basis of their full and effective participation in development.

8. Young people should play a leading role in the renewal of education by participation in the decision-making bodies of educational institutions, and also by direct action for the education of themselves and their fellows, both within the established forms of education and through new experiments;

9. Young people should be enabled to participate in health, welfare and other services aimed at helping their fellow men and, if necessary, new and unorthodox approaches should be adopted in the administration of these services to achieve this end;

10. There should be direct participation by youth in the decision-making process of the basic (grassroots) units of society—family, community, school and work. At higher levels of political, social, economic, and cultural institutions, their participation should take place on a representative basis;

11. The existing special schemes for youth training and employment should be subject to regular evaluation, to assess their contribution to the reduction of youth employment, to the welfare of individuals and to the benefit of society;

12. Youth and youth organizations should be supported in their efforts to mobilize public opinion in favor of development: the form of support should include the availability of relevant information in attractive formats and assistance toward the greater interchange of young people from developed areas of the world.

13. The United Nations and the specialized agencies should replace their present frequently overlapping and fragmented approach to youth programs by a real concerted effort involving co-ordination especially at the country and regional levels;

14. The United Nations Volunteer Program should increasingly see its objectives as being to encourage and support the participation of young volunteers in the development of their own country by participating in projects whether or not they are aided by United Nations technical assistance;

15. The United Nations should organize a second World Youth Assembly which should have the task of evaluating to what extent the proposals made at the first Assembly held in 1970 have been implementing the effective participation of youth in the Second Development Decade;

16. The United Nations and specialized agencies should be the first to apply the above principles about youth participation to their own structures, methods of work and relationships with youth and youth organizations. (United Nations, 1972c).

The second and harder step to be taken is to involve young adolescents and children under twelve in the planning process. This requires that adults cross age barriers to spend time with persons much younger than themselves. It requires that adults perceive and enter (*not* take over) the social spaces in the home, neighborhood and community where children carry out their great variety of unnoticed social, civic and economic roles. Only then will adults become aware of the whole range of fresh new perceptions about personhood and human potentiality and alternative modes of social problem-solving which exist in the hidden spaces of the child's world. Only by spending time in these spaces will adults begin to realize the burden placed on children and on society as a whole by present concepts of legal majority, so ill fitted to the living social reality of that half of the world's population labeled minors. And only by making the "adult only" spaces available to the younger members of the under twenty-one population will these younger members gain rapidly enough an understanding of the dilemmas and problems of the contemporary world and be able to bring their own insights and skills to bear on them. Deferring participation rights until youth are are in their twenties and thirties and older guarantees that they will never have the freshness of their own earlier insights left by the time they have decision-making power.

For these things to happen, new understandings of the nature of personhood at different ages, and of the interaction between social institutions, personhood and human productivity (in the broadest sense of the word) at different ages, have to be developed. The process of rewriting the Declaration of the Rights of Children and Youth, an important project to pursue during the International Year of the Child, will inevitably be a process of reexamining old concepts about childhood and youth, as well as about the middle and older years of life. This brings us back to the concept of the life cycle with which we started. Any reexamination of the status of children and youth and the possibilities of a new partnership between generations in shaping the future must be in the context of a perception of the unfolding whole of human life for each individual. Part III will deal with that context, and also look particularly at the role of the elderly in the intergenerational partnership.

NOTES

1. Blackstone is very explicit about this: "So that full age in male and female is twenty-one years, which age is completed on the day preceding the anniversary of a person's birth; who till that time is an infant, and so styled in law" (Ehrlich's Blackstone 98 (1959)).

2. Class action refers to legal action being taken with regard to any category of person, such as women, children, the elderly or specific ethnic or racial minorities, on the basis of membership in that category rather than on the basis of the individual's situation or need.
3. The term family as used here is not meant to apply only to family units consisting of husband, wife and biological, adopted or foster children. Single-parent households are also families, and in fact parentless children "raising" each other can also be a family. I refer here to a commitment over time to nurturance of others in a household setting, usually involving two generations (or more). There are also communal families, involving several sets of adults and children. These were more frequent in medieval Europe than they are today.
4. Absorption of parentless children into other families is done with much greater ease in nonindustrial socities.
5. PIE has submitted evidence to the Home Office Criminal Law revision Committee, which is reviewing the laws relating to sexual offences. It proposes the abolition of the age of consent, and the legalisation of sexual relationships between consenting children, and between consenting children and consenting adults. PIE's evidence argues that "the involvement of the police, court and press transforms private, tender and loving experiences into public parades of guilt, hate and retribution" . . . Children may be removed and put into care—which they see as punishment rather than protection. The adult can be imprisoned for long periods for what was a tender and loving relationship, harrassed by the police, prison wardens and other prisoners (Press release from Paedophile Information Exchange, published in *Peace News,* January 4, 1976.
6. The Behavior Today News Roundup for March 6, 1978 reports on a paedophilic bordello in the working class Boston suburb of Revere, where men had "more or less consensual" sex with young boys. ("They did it in Sparta," is the rationale.) Intergenerational sex is predicted by one Boston gay leader as the gay movement's next big issue.
7. The difficulty in developing a sufficiently objective and appropriately ameliorative public policy with regard to child abuse can be seen in the warning from a United States Civil Liberties Union Juvenile Rights Program that child abuse is becoming a fashionable cause warranting wholesale invasion of family privacy, and leading to maternity ward screening of new mothers as to their potentiality for child abuse (Uviller 1977).
8. The single most overwhelmingly supported research finding in regard to child abuse is that abusers are themselves the children of parents who were abusers, replicating an endless chain of intergenerational abuse. In this way are "the sins of the fathers visited on the third and fourth generation." See Davoren, Steele and Jolly (1975:2-9).
9. Other categories of diseases given in WHO statistics are not included in this table because they are of relatively minor importance, particularly in the third world. Industrial world degenerative diseases are not discussed in this paper. By and large these are not childhood diseases.
10. A recent United States survey of the nutritional knowledge of a sample of independent grocers, who by their own admission gave nutritional advice to customers on request, produced an average score just short of failing, on nine basic questions (Stansfield and Fox of the University of Nebraska, reported by Mayer and Dwyer 1977).

11. This may refer to accidents in home workshops and with farm machinery. In the United States, the more mechanized the farm, the higher the accident rate for persons of all ages, particularly children. Lost hands, arms, legs and lives are not an uncommon occurance among farm children.

12. A recent United States study found that 5.4 percent of all six to seventeen year old children were out of school (Children's Defense Fund Report 1974).

13. These are general guesstimates based on observation in several different third world school systems. I am indebted to my colleague Professor Richard Kraft in the University of Colorado School of Education for pointing out the extent both of the dropout and the return phenomena.

14. Even less encouraging are current (1977) reports from the National Assessment of Educational Progress that American teenagers are not good at making practical use of their skill with numbers and letters in ordinary everyday tasks.

15. For an overview of the problem of the young offender, see the following: United Nations (1965); Hinners (1973); Wilkerson (1973); Cavan (1968); Connor (1972); Lowenstein (1965); Clifford (1976); and Wakin (1975).

16 Cases brought to court in which a parent is denying medical attention to a child in urgent need of it, because of religious beliefs prohibiting medical intervention, are not infrequent. Sometimes the child or other family member wishes the medical aid to be given, yet the judge will rule for the parent, usually the mother, as the only person capable of protecting the best interests of the child. (For example, *Sampson* 317 N.Y.S. 2d 641 (1970); Hudson 126 P 2d 765 Washington (1942). In cases where parents simply do not provide a home for a child, the child may wind up in a juvenile detention home by default, having committed no deliquent act (Blakes 4 III, App. 3d at 572, 281 N.E. 2d at 457 (1972).

17. The following recent pathetic letter of a seventeen-year old to the Dear Abby advice column that appears in many United States newspapers illustrates the dilemma of many young women:

    Dear Abby: Please help me. Does a runaway seventeen-year-old girl have any rights? I have a five-month old baby and am living with a guy whom I care about very much. I also have a job and a roof over my head. I haven't been home since the baby was born for fear my parents would have my boyfriend arrested.

    I've heard that at seventeen there is nothing they can d   . .ing I am O.K. Is that true?

    Homesick and Worried

    Dear Homesick: Check with the Legal Aid Service listed in your telephone book. There you will get legally sound and confidential advice.

18. In some states females are given rights before males, in other states vice versa.

19. The right of young persons even *over* the age of twenty-one to choose their own religion is being hotly contested in a court battle in the United States at the time of this writing. A group of parents are asking for custody of their legally adult offspring to subject them to a program which is intended to make them abandon their religious beliefs (because they assert that these beliefs were coerced in their children). The first court judgement based on the sanctity of the family principle, was in favor of the parents against the children. The case is now being appealed.

20. Holt (1974), Foster (1974) and the United Nations Declaration of the Rights

of the Child have all been drawn on in this declaration. See the Appendix for each of these declarations in full, as well as the Youth Liberation Program of Ann Arbor. Also, compare the "One Kid's Own Bill of Rights" in the Appendix with the declaration offered here.

21. The difficulties reported on in implementing the Basic Services Program at the 1977 Manila Meeting (United Nation 1977c) may conceivably be related to the disproportionate number of men engaged in planning and administration. Women's skills and knowledge are consistently underused in UNICEF, and in other United Nations agencies, as they are elsewhere.

III.
The Life Span Approach

LOOKING AT THE LIFE CYCLE

In this section we bring together the materials already presented on the pathologies in social perception and social practice regarding children and youth, with fresh materials on the pathologies in social perception and social practice regarding the elderly. Custom, behavior and social structure combine to make "children" out of persons at both ends of the age span. Before going into detailed material on the situation of the elderly we will explore the life cycle concept itself, and the meanings for society of age differentiation and its ever present concomitant, gender differentiation. Once we have established the essential unity of human development over life span, a unity that persists in the face of all efforts at social segmentation, we will turn to the task of describing the elderly. The final sections will critically examine how age differentiation works in terms of the social roles available to the young and old, and we close with a look into a future in which the wise elder and the aware child have been incorporated into society.

Age is a unique sorting device for human beings, as compared to race, sex, class and ethnicity, in that every human being is or has been a child, and every human being moves through a biosocial succession of age statuses until cut off by death. Every human being who lives long enough experiences two minority statuses—the first of being a child, and the second of being old. Each has its own socially assigned limitations of opportunity. These limitations may be mitigated by membership in a favored gender, race, ethnic group or class, but they do not disappear. They may be much exacerbated by membership in nonfavored social categories. If we visualize all socially targeted minorities as being additionally subject to the universal sorting device of age, we see that certain groups in society carry a much heavier loading of minorityhood and its

101

attendant lack of control over the conditions of life than others. From a human rights standpoint, no form of minorityhood is acceptable. Here we are particularly concerned with the social use of age to create status.

In order to capture the full meaning of age as a human sorting device, we must look at the life cycle from birth to death, the wheel of life. In fact, we must look at the prebirth period, since all individual life cycles overlap their forebearers and (frequently) their successors in the great chain of social being. In the course of developing a model for age sorting over the life cycle, I realized that it was impossible to delineate age sorting without paying attention to a second sorting device which is also experienced by all human beings — the sorting by gender. Every human being receives one of two possible gender assignments at birth, and roughly every second human being experiences lifelong minority status due to the assignment of female gender. Like age-based minorityhood, the effects of gender may be mitigated or exacerbated depending on race, ethnic group or class membership, but the effects never completely disappear. All women, then, carry a double load of minority status in their younger and older years.

Life cycles intersect generationally for most people, though not for all, in a family. This is important because a person's family, or lack of one, is the first sorting device at birth which determines how heavily the minority statuses of age, gender and other possible categories will rest on an individual. Figure 1 represents schematically the conceptual model used in this part of our study. The individual is viewed as subject to a series of sorting processes from before conception to death, each of which in turn determines further life chances. The first of these sorting processes is set in motion by the level of industralization, and population, GNP and urbanization growth rates of the society into which an individual is born, which establish certain parameters for all other life chances. The SES (socio-economic status) of the household into which an individual is born, and its associated community linkage system and child-rearing practices, act as a further sorting device for individuals from the moment of conception. At the moment of birth, there is further sorting by gender, and gender-related life expectancy. Birth also involves, for both males and females, being sorting into the minority status of childhood, which lasts, in terms of legal status, until they are twenty-one.

Extent of gender role differentiation is relatively mild until puberty, when a sharp role differentiation takes place and lasts until about age fifty-five, when gender roles either converge or reverse. The next major sorting after puberty comes with entry into the labor force, into marriage, and into parenting, events that usually come within a relatively short time period for most individuals. For women, entry into the labor

Figure 1. Age and Gender Sorting of Human Beings Over the Life Cycle, with Prior Societal and Family Sorting Indicated

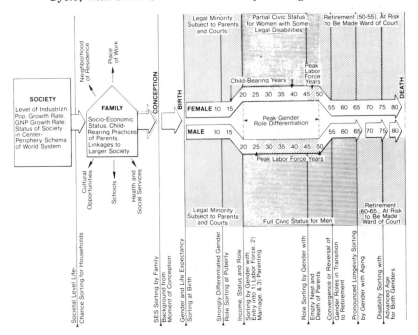

force involves a general determined income sorting; women command lower wages than men throughout life. Entry into marriage involves status re-sorting for women, as they (by tradition at least) take on the SES of their husbands. The latter's SES remains relatively unchanged from childhood, allowing for small movements upward or downward in the status scale as a result of personal achievement or disachievement. If there are remarriages, for women each marriage means a status re-sorting (if the new spouse's SES is different than the old); for men, status stays the same throughout successive marriages.[1] Entry into parenting involves major role shifts for women toward primary responsibility for child care, minor role shifts for men toward increasing involvement in the household.

Apt to be lost in the complex of role sortings that take place with entry into the labor force, marriage and parenting, is the sorting based on change in legal status that comes with reaching the twenty-first year of age. Full adulthood, involving contractual rights to dispose of one's person and property, comes for most young men after they have already entered into the adult responsibilities of work and marriage. In this sense women never attain full adulthood, although they may begin child-bearing, with or without spouse, at age fourteen or fifteen. There are varying degrees of lifelong legal constraints on their contractual rights in every part of the world. They do however attain a significant increase in rights at age twenty-one. The next major sorting for women comes at the close of the childbearing and rearing years, with the piling up of the phenomena of the empty next, illness and death of the couple's own parents, and reentry into the labor force, all of which occur within a short span of time. This is a period of release for women from the care of the young and the old. This role sorting process has minimal implications for men, whose labor force and household roles remain fairly stable from marriage to retirement.

The complex role sorting for women involved with the empty nest, death of parents and heavier labor force participation is followed, as retirement nears, by a gradual role convergence or actual role reversal for women and men. Noted in widely different cultural contexts, in societies with widely differing levels of industralization, this convergence involves women taking on behavioral characteristics ordinarily conceived as typically masculine, active, mastery-oriented. Men take on behavioral characteristics ordinarily conceived as typically feminine, passive, adaptive (Gutmann 1977). In nonindustrial societies, this stage is not accompanied by any formal retirement from the labor force, for either women or men, but by a gradual lessening of work load as declining strength dictates. In industrial societies, substantial sectors of the population, though not all, formally retire between the ages of fifty-five to seventy. Entry into the earlier stages of advanced aging processes become evident during this period. There is a noticeable longevity sorting by gender. At each age throughout the life span more males have died than females, but the greater risk of death for males becomes more pronounced at this time. Numbers of women enter into widowhood roles as men die. Disability sorting is also noticeable by the seventies, but here the sorting applies to survivors of both sexes. By this age, women and men alike are at risk of being deprived of the rights they gained at age twenty-one, and of once more being made into minors—this time as wards of the court, or wards of their own children. This rights deprivation may or may not be related to actual physical and mental incapacity.

Death brings the lifespan sequence with its differential sorting stations for women and men as they move from age to age, to an end. At the close of life, as at its inception, gender differentiation is minimal. Aging, for the first and last part of the lifespan, seems to be the primary sorting device. Only in the middle years does gender differentiation predominate. Because the middle years of life have been treated, at least in the West, as the only significant part of the human lifespan, the gender differentiation of this period may have been receiving more attention than it deserves. A clearer recognition that the human lifespan moves from the androgyny of the young to the androgyny of the old may help to bring more objective considerations to bear on the utility of the violent gender differentiation in the middle years of life.

Androgyny and the Life Span

What is androgyny? It means, partaking of the character of both the male and the female. Young persons before puberty have considerable freedom in all societies, including purdah-keeping societies, to move in a variety of social spaces and try out, in play, a variety of roles.[2] It is a period of easy friendship and camaraderie for girls and boys, both in same-sex groupings and cross-sex groupings. While girls who enjoy what are labelled as masculine activities too heartily may be called tomboys, and boys who enjoy what are labelled as feminine activities too much may be called sissies, there is a certain social permissiveness in indulging such preferences. In contemporary western societies this historical permissiveness has somewhat lost its force because of the powerful mass media reenforcement for imitating stereotyped adult same-sex models, but it nevertheless remains to some degree. In part, the efforts of the feminist movement to abolish sex stereotyping for children is helping to recreate an earlier freedom for the young.

With puberty this permissiveness is withdrawn, and the easy cross-sex friendships of ten-year-olds turn into selfconcious cross-sex sparring between fourteen-year-olds. Sex stereotyping is a serious business, and girls who at younger ages might have aspired to be doctors or firemen when they grew up now know (or did, before recent efforts at reforming sex stereotyping in textbooks) that they are supposed to be nurses or teachers. Ways of carrying the body, dressing, gesturing and speaking become sharply differentiated between young female and male teenagers, except in the unisex subculture which deliberately defies this differentation process.

Striking as these behavioral changes are, it is worth noting that it is only from puberty to menopause (and its male equivalent) that each person is socially restricted to gender role behavior appropriate to that gender. While there are departures from the norm, during this period aggressive females and nurturant males are not as highly valued as nurturant females and aggressive males. Some time in the fifties, or perhaps not until retirement (in societies that invoke this category), there is a role reversal (Gutman 1977). Women move from passive to active mastery while the men move in the opposite direction. Often the wife and older son pair up to take control of their father and the rest of the family. Women's lifelong repertoire of adaptive skills, and especially their social bonding skills, put them at an advantage in any moves and any new situations that must be met in the later years. Where older women, particularly widowed women, move to the city to seek new challenges, and to find new members of old kin networks, older men return to the country to redevelop familiar parts of old kin networks. Where older men suffer from loss of former role and status, women are used to teasing as many dimensions as possible out of an initially thin role, and having to make do with inferior status. Reduction of domestic responsibilities with the empty nest and death of aged parents gives them new freedom to work at role creation. Addition of domestic responsibilities for older men gives them new experiences of active nurturance roles. Older men"rule,"to the extent that they do, by force of ascribed authority and knowledge of power systems; women "rule" by the force of an expanding social experience and knowledge of human nature. This force of older women is in fact sometimes feared in a society, and measures will be taken to control her power, such as labeling her a witch.

Gender-role maturation for women then means moving from (1) androgyny with socialization for femininity to (2) full feminine role to (3) feminine role transformed with the aid of a strong masculine component. For men the same sequence involves (1) androgyny with socialization for masculinity, (2) full masculine role and (3) masculine role transformed with the aid of a strong feminine component. One might characterize both sexes as moving, in the ideal sequence, from an undifferentiated androgyny to a differentiated androgyny over a lifetime. A fuller awareness of this process may be the key to reducing inappropriate gender-based role assignments.[3]

AGE DIFFERENTIATION

The Social Meaning of Age

Since aging has clearcut physiological concomitants, so that one has no difficulty in distinguishing the young from the middle-years person from the old, it is perhaps somewhat surprising that the more a society undergoes what is known as "modernization" the further that society departs from age categorizations based on physiological and developmental characteristics. Since it is the "modern" societies, primarily Western, that are supplying categories and methodologies for the application of human rights concepts to human beings of various ages and conditions, the age-sorting to be described in this part of our study, even though it conforms neither to traditional usage nor to physiological reality, is increasingly being adopted as national practice in all societies as part of the "modernization" process. The sorting process that divides human beings into under twenty-fives,[4] twenty-five to fifty-five-year olds, and over fifty-fives, is a process that has been uniquely useful to one group of modernizing countries in Euro-North America in the latter part of the last century, and in this century. Through mandatory school-

Table 15. Age categories in Common Usage

A. PRE-ADULTHOOD, 0-24

    0-4   Children, no labor force responsibility

    5-9   Children, LICs: moderate labor force responsibility, some schooling.

           MICs: schooling only.

    10-14   Adolescents, LICs: increasing labor force responsibility, some schooling.

           MICs: schooling only.

    15-19   Youth, LICs: full labor force participation.

           MICs: increasing labor force participation.

    20-24   Young adults, LICs and MICs: Full legal majority for men, but limitations on civic participation.

           Limited legal majority for women, limited civic participation.

B. FULL-ADULTHOOD, PRIME OF LIFE, 25-55

    25-55   LICs and MICs: For men, no legal limitations.

           For women, some limitations on rights to make contracts, buy, sell and administer property.

C. RETIREMENT STATUS, 56--

    56-64   Period of preparation for withdrawal from prime of life status, beginning of gradual withdrawal from labor force in MICs; adaptive reduction in work load in LICs.

    65-74   The young elderly, active retirement life style established in MICs; adaptation of work load, development of role of wise elder in LICs.

    75+   The aged elderly, development of nursing care as needed, and according to the social class of the elderly in MICs; wise elder role, nursing care, or abandonment, according to custom in LICs.

MICs = More Industrialized Countries

LICs = Less Industrialized Countries

ing it upgraded the skill of the next generation's labor power while withholding it from the labor market as a competitive, lower-cost source of labor. Through retirement it also excluded the competition of cheap elderly laborers. In each age group, as we shall see, women have been further differentially excluded (as have ethnic, racial and class minorities). Other approaches to upgrading labor skills and spreading labor requirements over a large share of the population have been considered antiprogressive in capitalist societies, although various socialist societies have experimented with alternative patterns. The three ages concept, however, with labor requirements being largely met by the middle years population, has tended to operate as an ideal in socialist as well as capitalist societies. The series of age categories in Table 8, which I have constructed as a summation of the most common usage in literature on youth and age in international contexts, offers an overview of the three stages concept as it exists in the twentieth century.[4]

We have already explored in detail in Part I and Part II the minority status of persons under twenty-one. However, it is one thing for the young, who have never known any other condition, to experience the powerlessness of minority status. It is quite another thing for the old, who have once been powerful, to experience that minority status. Alexander (1975:268) writes about the entry for the elderly into a managed state after a life of freedom, with restricted rights to manage their own property, to determine their life style, and how "it is at once more shocking and more terrible because it is unaccustomed." Much of the power loss of the elderly relates to drastically reduced income, and associated reduction of life style choices. Other power losses refer to loss of status with the loss of job, particularly severe for men because their social identity and their job identity are one. The disinclination of the community to give important civic roles to retirees reenforces the sense of status loss. The most severe power loss of all, however, is to have the court appoint a guardian to manage one's affairs, an event that may occur to an elderly person with as much decision-making capacity as many middle-years persons whose right to manage their affairs is never contested. With age, the elderly person's judgement in business and personal affairs becomes subject to scrutiny in ways that would be considered an unwarranted invasion of privacy between the ages of twenty-five and sixty-five.[5]

Loss of power of course is relative to social class. In fact, the onset of aging is more a matter of class definition than of biology. For the working classes, aging begins at forty-five; few are considered hireable after a job loss at that age; for the middle class it is between fifty-five and sixty-five, and for the upper class it can be postponed for a long time — sometimes into the eighties. Income differentials increase sharply for the elderly. The rich get richer, the poor get much poorer. Women are the poorest of all, and live the longest in their poverty.

The characteristics of all the old and young, and their untapped potentials for social participation, will be explored more fully in the next section. We will see that the "powerful" suffer as much as the "powerless" from the exclusion of the young and old from the work force and from civic participation.

MATURATION PROCESSES FROM YOUTH TO AGE

The three stages concept of the life cycle, in its emphasis on presence or absence of rights and status, masks the rich developmental processes that unfold from childhood to old age. In fact, the social attitudes toward childhood and old age imply that persons in these age categories have nothing of importance to contribute to society. The sections that follow are intended to show how false those implications are, and how impoverishing for the societies that act on these attitudes.

Developmental Strengths of the Young

Briefly to review the discussion from Parts I and II, basic intellectual capacities are present very young in children. Complex moral and political reasoning can take place at least by the age of twelve if not younger. The ages from ten to fourteen appear to be a period during which children's cognitive capacities and social intuitions produce creative new social responses which may remain cut off from the world of adults. Least noticed of all, children enrich the lives of adults through play. The child in the family is the provider of creative and playful activity which adults have lost the capacity to engage in alone. The low status of playful and creative activity in the community reenforces the low status of the child that engages in it, and renders increasingly inaccessible this recreative activity for persons of all ages.

Developmental Strengths of the Elderly

The loss of functioning findings based on cross-sectional studies of performance by age are now being questioned by longitudinal studies which do not show these decrements in functioning. Rather they show an increase with aging in what intelligence tests call "crystallized intelligence," measuring acculturational skills, and in visualization, the ability to organize and process visual materials, even in the period from age seventy to seventy-seven (Barton, et al. 1975:224-236). The aged like

everyone else vary in performance capacity according to the genetic ability, educational level, life experience, health and current circumstances,
but evidence seems to be increasingly clear that on the average the elderly
keep growing in certain areas of mental functioning until death. Personality differentiation also continues until death. The much noted
withdrawl phenomenon associated with aging has to be seen in the context of need to protect the self from enviromental and social stress, and
also as a shift in value priorities according to new insights.[6] The ancient
wisdom of East and West about the withdrawl into the forest to ponder
the nature of humanity and the social order after children have been
reared appears to arise independently at the appropriate time in the life
cycle, in widely differing types of societies. The withdrawl is rarely complete, but involves a gentle rhythm of withdrawl and return, withdrawl
and return, in the closing years of life. We know little about the quality
and content of intergeneration relations in societies with this rhythm,
and know even less about how to cope with the emergence of that rhythm
in our own society. We see only the statics of withdrawl, not the pulsing
movement of back and forth. Recognizing the back and forth is vital to
our own survival, for the elderly, knowing more of the past, may have
more wide-ranging views of the future than those who have lived a
shorter time. The elderly are often more optimistic than the young. It
might be important to find out why.[7]

The specific intellecting capacities of the young and old, each at their
own kind of biosocial peak, are important for society. The different
capacities for social construction based on the most recent first-hand experience of social reality in the young, and the oldest accessible experience of social reality in the old, may be equally crucial in dealing with
a time of systems break, when current modes of social operation and
problem solving may be wildly inappropriate.

THE EFFECTS OF INDUSTRIALIZATION ON
AGE DIFFERENTIATION

Certain types of human experience appear to be very widespread if not
universal, such as the experience of gender-role development for both
sexes. Other types of experiences are markedly different as between industrial and nonindustrial societies. These differences are most clear with
respect to the extent to which the two types of societies involve the young
and the old in major economic and social responsiblities. Figure 2 is a
schematic representation of the participation of old and young in industrial and nonindustrial societies. (The data base for this graph comes
in Table 19) Figure 3 is a schematic representation of the status of the aged as societies modernize, based on the Palmore and Manton Equality

Index (Palmore and Manton 1974). The work load is spread more evenly across the total life span in nonindustrial societies. With industrialization there is an increasing restriction of the social space of the elderly, and a heavy loading of economic and social responsiblity on a narrow age range. Only among the well-to-do is there a status and participation curve similar to that of the nonindustrial societies for the elderly. For the middle classes, aging is usually considered to begin at fifty-five, an increasingly "popular" retirement age. For the working classes, aging begins at forty-five. Past that age an unemployed worker finds great difficulty in being rehired. Given that youth is generally not totally integrated into the labor force before eighteen or twenty, and not given major responsibility, either on the job or in civic roles, before twenty-five, we have the phenomenon of much of the society's work being done by persons between the ages of twenty-five and fifty-five, a preponderance of them men.

The rates at which all parts of the world's population are aging and the greater longevity of women than men, suggest that this pattern, if followed by parts of the world now becoming industrialized, would place an increasingly heavy burden on middle years males. Table 16, showing the current and estimated distribution of first and third world populations among these age groups, helps us to understand how differently the burdens of the middle class folk are patterned in the more and less industrialized countries. In Asia, Africa an Latin America the population under twenty-five ranges from 53.8 percent in East Asia to 62.4 percent in Africa. They have few folk over fifty-five—from seven to ten percent of their populations. In Europe and North America there are fewer under twenty-five—forty to forty-five percent, and more older folk—eighteen to twenty percent. The middle-years population differs in size for the more and less industrialized countries. The more industrialized world has nearly forty percent of its middle-years population in the work force, the less industrialized world closer to thirty percent. Table 17, giving the United Nations estimates of the proportion of persons over sixty between now and 2000 for the two worlds, shows the impending aging of both sets of populations by the year 2000, though much more so for the more than the less industrialized. More industrialized countries will have their population over sixty increase from 11.3 percent in 1950 to 15.9 percent by 2000. Less industrialized countries will have their population increase from 5.6 percent in 1950 to 7.0 percent by 2000. Neither set of countries can afford to leave their old and their young out of active partnership in the decades to come. The middle third of the population has not coped well with the crises of the twentieth century, and they need help.

Figure 2. Schematic Representation of Participation by Age in Labor Force in Industrialized and Non-Industrialized Societies

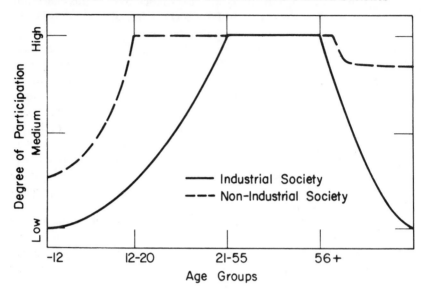

Figure 3. Schematic Representation of Status of the Aged by Degree of Modernization

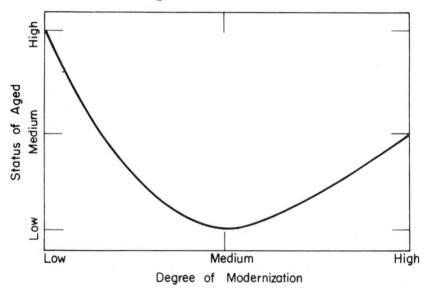

Table 16. Composition of the Population of the World and Major Areas by Age-Group, Estimates for 1960

Table 16. Composition of the Population of the World and Major Areas by Age-Group, Estimates for 1960.

Age	World[a,b,c] Total	East Asia[a]	South Asia[b]	Europe	Soviet Union	Africa	North America	Latin America	Oceania[c]
% Population Age 0-25	53.5	53.8	59.3	40.3	46.9	62.4	45.0	60.2	46.4
% Population Age 25-55	35.2	35.9	32.9	39.4	39.1	30.6	37.4	31.8	37.9
% Population Age 55+	11.3	10.3	7.8	20.3	14.0	7.0	17.6	8.0	15.7

[a]Not including North Korea and the Ryukyu Islands.

[b]Not including Israel and Cyprus.

[c]Not including Polynesia and Micronesia.

SOURCE: United Nations (1964:Table II, Appendix B).

Table 17. Actual and Estimated Proportions of the World Population, Age 60 Years and Over, for More Industrialized and Less Industrialized Countries

Region	Year	Percent of Total Population
World	1950	7.6
	1970	8.0
	1985	8.2
	2000	9.0
More Industrialized Countries	1950	11.3
	1970	14.1
	1985	14.8
	2000	15.9
Less Industrialized Countries	1950	5.6
	1970	5.4
	1985	6.0
	2000	7.0

SOURCE: United Nations (1975a:22, Table 7).

Since problems of age and gender differentiation will be unequally felt by different parts of the world, the remainder of this study will present comparative data on participation of the young and old for the same fifteen countries studied in Part I. Table 18 gives the age distribution of the population in these fifteen countries, so we can see the specific situation of individual countries as compared to regional totals in Table 9. In Africa, Asia (save Japan) and Latin American the population under twenty-four is between fifty-nine and sixty-five percent, the over fifty-fives are from seven to fourteen percent, and the middle-years population is between twenty-six and thirty percent. The middle-years population does not reach a third of the total in any of these countries, and if we did not know how many under twenty-fours were in the work force we would wonder how these societies could manage. In Euro-North America and Japan the picture is very different. The under twenty-fours are much fewer, thirty-four to forty-four percent, the elderly are relatively more frequent, from nineteen percent in Spain to twenty-seven percent in Sweden, and the middle-years population is almost the same in every country, varying only between thirty-six and thirty-nine percent. They represent comfortably more than a third of the population. We note that the third world countries with the smallest middle-years work force are also the countries with the highest population growth rates, from 2.5 to 3.5 over the eight-year period from 1965 to 1973, so their burden will continue to grow. No western country was growing at more than 1.1 percent during that period. Japan, the modernized Asian country that belongs to the first world demographically and economically, had a growth rate of 1.2 during that time. The sheer difference in proportions of middle years to young and old must be constantly borne in mind in thinking of the situation of the first and third ages of life as between more and less industrialized countries.

AGE DIFFERENTIATION AND SOCIAL ROLES

Employment of the Young and the Old

One of the supposed blessings of modernization has been the removal of the necessity to work for the young and the old. Yet no welfare-oriented state, no matter how affluent, has been able to provide adequately for the economic needs at the two ends of the age spectrum, nor has it been able to offer fully satisfying alternatives to economic production roles. The school dropout rates in the United States, beginning in elementary school, suggest the inadequacy of schools as the main focus of life for the young. The bitterness of many on-the-shelf retirees suggest the inadequacy of workload removal as the focus of life for the old. The move to abolish mandatory retirement ages in the very western countries that pioneered to establish retirement status leaves no doubt about the change in attitudes of senior citizens in regard to retirement. The right to remain in the labor force as long as an individual desires is an important human right now generally acknowledged. The assignment of minority status to the young and to the old, with legal restrictions on their activities and the attendant possibilities of employing the young and the old at substandard wages, has led to exploitation, poverty and misery for both groups.

Comparative information about wage scales by age is not available, so in the analysis that follows only presence or absence from the labor force is documented. The fact that under-twenties and over sixty-fives are paid less than the middle-years work force is indirectly demonstrated by Figure 4 which shows the disproportionate number of under-twenty-twos and over-sixty-fives at the poverty level in the United States. The under twenty-twos include children as well as the employed young, and the over-sixty-fives include both employed elders and pensioners.

Table 18. Economic and Social Variables

	Africa			Asia		
	Egypt	Algeria	Tanzania	Japan	Philip-pines	Thailand
% Population under Age 24[a]	59.0	63.7	60.2	39.5	62.9	63.7
% Population Age 25-54[a]	26.5	26.9	30.6	44.6	29.6	26.5
% Population Age 55+[a]	14.5	9.2	9.1	15.9	8.0	7.2
Population Growth Rate, 1965-1973[b]	2.5	3.4	2.8	1.2	3.0	3.0
Population in Centers under 20,000[c]	52.0	73.5	94.9	24.3	36.8	91.2
GNP Per Capita[b]	250	570	130	3,630	280	270
Economic Growth Rate, 1965-1973[b]	0.8	4.3	2.6	9.6	2.6	4.5

[a] Yearbook of Labor Statistics (United Nations, 1976f:Table 1).

[b] Boulding Global Data Bank.

[c] Boulding, Carson, Nuss and Greenstein (1976).

There are enormous differences in patterning of employment by age and sex from country to country, even within the same region, and yet also certain similarities. The most striking similarity across culture regions and development zones is the disparity in employment of women as compared to men, although this disparity does not apply at all ages.[8] Reminding ourselves first about the situation of the young, we see from Table 19 that countries from all regions report some employment of under-fifteens. One-half to two-thirds of fifteen to nineteen-year-old males are in the work force in all regions, working at a time when they are still legally children and have no contractual rights. Teenage women are employed at close to the same rate as men or higher in Tanzania and Thailand, and in Hungary, Sweden and the United Kingdom. Elsewhere employment of teenage women ranges from four percent in Moslem North Africa to nearly fifty percent in the United States. The large numbers of teenage women not in the labor force are either unpaid family laborers or mothers rearing their own children.

If we compare the work load carried by the disfranchised old, the over sixty-fives, the differences between industrial and nonindustrial societies are very great. including gender differences. In Euro-North America, only twelve to twenty percent of men over sixty-five are in the work force.

Table 18 (cont'd)

	Euro–North America						Latin America		
France	Hungary	Sweden	Spain	United Kingdom	United States		Colombia	Mexico	Peru
39.9	37.5	34.0	43.2	38.6	43.9		64.7	65.1	62.8
35.7	39.0	38.9	37.9	36.2	36.3		38.2	27.2	28.9
24.5	23.5	27.1	18.9	25.0	19.8		7.1	7.7	8.1
0.8	0.3	0.7	1.1	0.4	1.0		2.8	3.5	2.9
58.1	58.2	55.8	54.6	16.6	53.0		43.0	70.4	64.8
4,540	1,850	5,910	1,710	3,060	6,200		440	890	620
5.0	2.7	2.4	5.3	2.3	2.5		3.1	2.8	1.8

In the rest of the world, from one-third to over three-fourths of men are still working. Only the women drop way back compared to earlier participation, though third world older women are much more in the labor force than first world women.

Table 19 also shows the percentage of men and women employed in the age period of peak employment for each sex in each country. There is a little variation for the men. There are recorded peaks in the mid-forties for men in three non-industrialized countries, but in most countries men between the ages of thirty and fourty-four are carrying the peak employment load in the enumerated labor force. For women the peak load varies widely, with the clustering at ages twenty to twenty-four, mainly in the third world, and another clustering at ages forty-five to fifty, for both Europe and the third world. The ages twenty-five to forty-five are the prime childbearing and childrearing ages. The youthful women's labor force is a low status group because of inexperience, and the older women's labor force is low status group because the mid-years' career of childbearing does not accumulate seniority in the job world. It would be interesting to know the reason for the greater rates of leaving the labor force for women after sixty-five, considering that the entry to the labor force has already been so late, in the mid-forties. Whether the leaving is voluntary or involuntary is not clear.

The early leaving may have something to do with the character of the occupations available. Table 20 shows the six most frequent occupations for men and for women in the United States, for over-sixty-fives.

Figure 4. Persons Below the Low-Income Level, by Age:
1959-71, U.S.A.

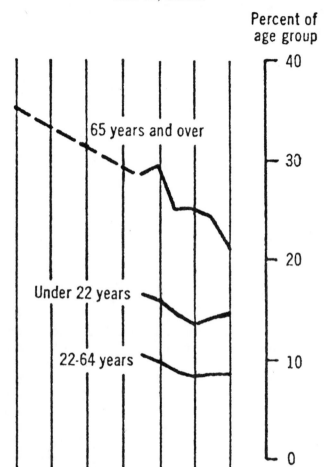

Household and service work may not seem very attractive after sixty-five. One of the group of women who do stay on in the labor force are women professionals, and they stay on in greater numbers than their male counterparts. (12.9 percent of over-sixty-five employed women are professionals, while only 8.4 percent of over-sixty-five employed men are professionals.) Early leaving for women also has something to do with the fact that the norms about retirement in some countries mandate earlier retirement for women than men, as Table 21 suggests. The United Kingdom and Hungary for example, require that women retire five years

earlier than men. Given the different attitudes toward aging and retirement on the part of women and men mentioned earlier, women in com-
fortable circumstances might prefer the freedom to organize their own
time outside the work force, and to rely on the kin network for social and
economic support. However, available evidence indicates that poverty
hits older women much harder than older men, particularly in industrial
societies, where they also live much longer. Women may be more
restricted than men from seeking employment by age rules or pension
regulations, although both sexes are handicapped in employment by age.
Women are also more likely to be in demand for home care and nursing
of spouses or other relatives.

Family Role Transitions for the Young and the Old

While legal age of marriage for women varies from twelve in Spain,
Colombia and Peru to eighteen in Sweden and the United States, the
years between fifteen and nineteen years of age see a significant role transition for many young women in all parts of the world as they enter marriage, consensual unions (not recorded) and motherhood in and out of
wedlock. We are reminded in Table 22 of what we saw in Parts I and II
that for most of the third world, from one-third to one-half of young
adult women marry during this period. The same is true for some first
world countries, including Hungary and the United States. In others, like
Sweden, as few as seven percent marry that young. The United States has
one of the highest rates of birth for young adult mothers in the world,
Japan the lowest. The sorting that take place with marriage and motherhood creates special roles for women besides labor force roles that they
carry until menopause. The counterpart roles for men involve primarily
labor force with some parenting.

If the teens are the years of family formation, the sixties and the seventies are the years of family dissolutions as spouses die, separate or
divorce. Widowhood is the primary sorting experience at this age. In
most countries during these decades divorce accounts for only one to
three percent of marital dissolutions.[9] (Tanzania is an exception. Divorce
accounts for twenty-eight percent of marital dissolutions.) The role convergence that develops as retirement nears helps both sexes deal with the
special and demanding role of self-sufficient widowhood. This is a type
of role that previous life experiences prepare neither sex for. Both asser-
tive and nurturant social capacities are required to create a new live-alone
life style (or new patterns of later years remarriage or consensual
unions). Legal and financial disabilities for elderly live alones and remar-
rieds may be as severe as the legal and the financial disabilities of young
adult parents. The elderly often avoid remarrying to avoid loss of

Table 19. Participation Labor Force by Sex and Age: Under 15s, Peak Age Employment and Over 65s

Employment Age Group	Africa			Asia		
	Egypt	Algeria	Tanzania	Japan	Philippines	Thailand
% Men Under 15	9.6	2.0	6.5	---	5.7	10.1
% Women Under 15	1.1	0.6	6.6	---	3.6	11.7
% Men, 16-19	49.0	65.7	59.3	23.0	52.4	77.4
% Women, 16-19	4.2	37.7	65.5	22.6	31.5	77.2
% Men at Peak Employment Age						
15-19	---	---	---	---	---	---
20-24	---	---	---	---	---	---
25-29	---	96.2	---	---	---	---
30-44	98.4*	---	---	98.7	90.5	96.5
45-49	---	---	95.9	---	---	---
% Women at Peak Employment Age						
15-19	---	37.7	---	---	---	---
20-24	9.7	---	---	66.8	---	---
25-29	---	---	---	---	---	---
30-44	---	---	---	---	---	---
45-49	---	---	80.1	---	38.7	79.6
% Men Over 65	38.6	33.3	79.6	49.5	56.5	44.6
% Women Over 65	0.7	1.4	42.0	15.5	17.7	21.2

*Refers to age group 30-49.

#No over 65 reported; percentage men employed at 60-64 is 74.9; percentage women employed at 60-64 is 30.0.

Source: United Nations (1975f).

testamentary rights to their property, or of pension rights. Increasingly, in countries where such loss of rights threaten, the elderly are choosing consensual unions rather than remarriage.

Educational programs, which might serve as social balancers by offering educational opportunities at the interim, non-peak load times in the life cycle for women and for men, rarely work that way, although there are exceptions. France has perhaps been the most successful with its invention of the Université du Troisième Age (University of the Third Age) by Professor Pierre Vellas at Toulouse in 1973. The idea has spread, and there are now approximately fifty such "universities" for older people operating around the world.[10] Another approach to education which actually involves elder persons in the production of knowledge, is the oral history movement by which the memories of the aged are collected and made available for future generations. "Ordinary persons" can be generators of historical texts simply by remembering how everyday life was for them in their younger years. This development, which has grown rapidly in North America, is also growing in other continents (Frontiers 1977). A special feature of oral history is that children and young people

Table 19 (cont'd)

| | Euro-North America | | | | | | Latin America | | |
France	Hungary	Sweden	Spain	United Kingdom	United States	Colombia	Mexico	Peru
---	0.3	---	2.2	---	---	7.2	2.2	1.6
---	0.9	---	1.1	---	---	4.0	0.9	1.3
42.8	45.8	56.5	65.9	60.8	60.6	54.1	59.9	39.8
31.3	49.1	52.2	36.7	55.7	49.0	25.1	20.9	17.7
---	---	---	---	---	---	---	---	---
---	---	---	---	---	---	---	---	---
---	98.5	---	---	---	---	---	---	---
97.0	---	95.8	96.8	98.2	95.6	92.7	---	---
---	---	---	---	---	---	---	93.9	97.1
---	---	---	---	---	---	---	---	---
---	---	---	39.6	---	---	32.4	24.1	25.8
---	---	---	---	---	---	---	---	---
---	69.7	---	---	---	---	---	---	---
45.5	---	77.9	---	61.5	55.6	---	---	---
19.3	---#	12.6	21.4	19.3	20.8	61.8	70.4	61.5
8.2	---#	3.6	3.9	6.3	7.8	13.8	10.9	8.5

are often involved in recording the knowledge of the elderly. (Note for example the Foxfire books 1975, 1977).

In general, however, education continues to be for youth. Most young people struggle to finish their education by age eighteen or twenty, if not earlier, often loading parenthood and labor force participation on top of schooling activities. Only 8.3 percent of persons over seventeen years of age participate in adult education programs in the United States, for example, and the majority of these persons are concentrated in their late teens and early twenties. Only 1.5 percent of all participants in adult education programs are over sixty-five. This is particularly sad since illiteracy rates are higher among the over sixty-fives, who passed through school-age years at a time when availabiltiy and length of schooling was drastically limited compared to today (*Social Indicators* 1973:110.) Forced to compete with younger persons who have different rhythms of learning, and often working under pressure, the elderly do not find adult education programs a source of pleasure, but rather one more source of insecurity. The many things the elderly could teach remain undiscovered by the young. There are signs that the tide is beginning to turn in some industrial countries, however, as agricultural and artisan skills now scarce among the young are being found among the elderly.

Table 20. Rank Ordering of Six Most Frequent Occupations, by Sex, of Employed Persons 65 and Over, U.S.A.

	Male Workers			Female Workers	
R A N K	Occupations	% Employed Persons of This Age Group in These Occupations	R A N K	Occupations	% Employed Persons of This Age Group in These Occupations
1	Farmers	15.9	1	Private and Household Workers	19.4
2	Craftsmen	14.3	2	Service Workers	15.5
3	Managers	13.8	3	Clerical	13.9
4	Professionals	8.4	4	Professional	12.9
5	Sales	8.2	5	Operatives	10.4
6	Clerical	6.2	6	Sales	8.8

SOURCE: Riley and Foner (1968:50).

Inequality in Misery and Death

The greatest age and gender-related inequalities are found in illness, death from all causes, and suicide rates.[11] Not until age sixty-five (in some countries age fifty-five) is an age cohort as susceptible again to fatal illness as it was in infancy. Tables 23A and 23B show what a heavy share of the burden of economic inequality and associated malnutrition and morbidity is borne by infants. The heaviest burden is borne by third world newborns. In Egypt, for example, 11156.6 infants die of each 100,000 born. The toll is considerably less in the industrialized world. Sweden has the lowest infant death rate, only 950 deaths per 100,000 born. A surprisingly heavy burden is nevertheless borne by newborns in countries like the United States (1771.8 infant deaths per 100,000 liveborn), United Kingdom (1687.5 infant deaths per 100,000 liveborn), and Hungary (3383.6 infant deaths per 100,000 liveborn). For the United States and the United Kingdom, these high infant death rates come from the internal third world of the poor. Survivors of that dangerous first year are given a brief respite from age one to fourteen, with the period from five to fourteen being the safest age they will ever know, in every country in the world. Death rates then climb slowly from fifteen to forty-four and then leap upwards from forty-five until death. Death rates take longer to leap in the first world, since inequality in longevity is one of the major inequalities between first and third worlds.

Table 21. Normal Retirement Age for Men and Women

Country	Normal Retirement Age	
	Women	Men
France	65	65
Hungary	55	60
Sweden	67	67
Spain	65	65
United Kingdom	60	65
United States	65	65

*According to public policy.

SOURCE: United Nations (1975a:33, Table 9).

The other most persistent inequality besides the heavy share of deaths among infants in every society, is the gender differential in death rates at every age in most countries. An inspection of the male and female death rates will show that more males than females die at every age from infancy on, in every country studied except Egypt, Colombia, Mexico and Peru. Only in the severer third world conditions is women's mortality higher, and then only at the two ends of the age spectrum. If there is genetic programing to protect the female of the species, it is a programming that lasts well into old age, long beyond the procreative years. What combination of genetic predispostion and differential social and physical stress produces this widespread effect is not yet understood.

Differential social stress would appear to be at work in generating the next major inequality, which is the differential suicide rate. Generally, suicide rates are much higher in the first world than in the third world,

Table 22. Youth and Age: Teen Years Marriage and Birth Rates, Elderly Widowhood Rates

	Africa			Asia			
	Egypt	Algeria	Tanzania	Japan	Philip-pines	Thailand	France
Women Under 20							
Legal Age of Marriage for Women ^{f}	16	---	---	16	14	---	15
Marriage Rates 15-19 ^{g}	48.6	52.3	---	34.5	36.9	---	19.7
Births Per Woman 15-19 ^{f}	.1921	.1276	---	.0122	.0772	.0831	.0635
Over 65, Both Sexes							
% Widowed 65-69 ^{h}	---	45.5 ^{abc}	14.6	32.9	---	32.7	24.1
% Widowed 70-74 ^{h}	---	---	23.9	45.0	---	49.3	36.0
% Widowed 75+ ^{h}	---	---	29.3	65.9	---	---	57.9

^{a}1971 Demographic Yearbook (United Nations, 1971a:Table 12).

^{b}Includes data for ages 65+.

^{c}Divorced and separated are combined.

^{d}Widowed and divorced are combined.

and men's rates are much higher than women's, as we see from Tables 24A and 24B. A leap in suicide rates from the under-fifteens to the fifteen to twenty-four-year-olds in Euro-North America and Asia is notable. Lack of suicide figures for Africa leave us unable to guess whether they would be high as in Asia or as low as reported in Latin America.[12] In Asia, women's suicide rates are much closer to men's than in Europe. They are actually higher for teenage women than men in Thailand, where women and men participate in the labor force at the same rates (see Table 19) — a grim foreboding of the consequences of equality of labor force participation for women in society structured as we now know it. Nowhere do we see more clearly the generalized stress involved in entering marriage, childbearing and labor force responsibilities in a concentrated brief period of time for teenagers than in the jump in suicide rates for this age group. What happens after the teenage jump varies between first and third worlds. In Euro-North America there is a general climb from age fifteen to death, with a second jump in rates after age forty-five. The same is true for Japan. In Thailand the rates decline after age twenty-four. The two suicide jumps associated with entry into and exit from the world of work and householding suggest how painful youth and age can be.

Table 22 (cont'd)

	Euro–North America				Latin America		
Hungary	Sweden	Spain	United Kingdom	United States	Colombia	Mexico	Peru
14	18	12	16	18	12	14	12
38.2	7.0	12.9	25.8	32.8	35.2	40.8	27.7
.1487	.0486	.0278	.1021	.2536	.1115	---	.1187
27.5	18.5^a	---	24.3^d	24.2	26.7^{ae}	21.9^e	---
40.0	27.9^a	---	36.7^d	33.9	33.4^{ae}	26.7^e	---
61.3	46.7^a	---	56.5^d	52.2	43.8^{ae}	34.9^e	---

[e]Marriage rates do not include "consensually married."
[f]Boulding, Nuss, Carson, Greenstein (1976).
[g]1973 Demographic Yearbook (United Nations, 1974a).
[h]1973 Demographic Yearbook (United Nations, 1974a).

It would not be possible to construct tables showing the relative amounts of illness suffered by women and men at different ages, but we are all aware that one of the concomitants of aging is increased ill health. Ill health can be both cause and effect of other problems of the elderly. It is inextricably interwoven with problems of unemployment, forcible retirement, poverty, poor housing and lack of civic roles. Adequate health care for the elderly is an important and acknowledged human right that is more honored in the breach than in the observance. Inadequate diet is a particular hazard for the elderly, due partly to poverty and partly to difficulties in procuring and preparing food. The net result is that the elderly in all countries are as vulnerable to disease as third world young children. Malnutrition is a particularly intractable problem for the elderly, because even when income and the ability to procure and prepare food are not in question, neither folk knowledge nor the knowledge of trained physicians about food needs of seniors — substantially different from the food needs of younger persons — can guide elders to a good use of available food resources. Substandard housing is another special hazard. Sheer lack of adequate heating in living quarters contributes to the premature death of older people from hypothermia — severely lowered body temperature.

Table 23A. Death Rates Specific for Sex and Age, Per 100,000 Population (Infant Deaths Per 100,000 Live-Born) (Asia and Latin America)

Country	Sex	All Ages	0	1-4	5-14	15-24	25-34	35-44	45-54	55-64	65-74	75+
Egypt	T	1375.6	11156.6	2473.6	184.5	241.3	238.2	391.0	892.2	2006.4	6113.2	19889.2
	M	1381.0	10536.6	2135.3	202.2	284.2	304.5	498.6	1191.5	2727.4	7592.9	15820.0
	F	1370.1	11822.2	2831.2	165.4	195.7	179.2	280.4	593.8	1302.7	3790.8	23233.1
Japan	T	652.6	1132.1	98.5	35.4	82.2	105.1	213.5	443.2	1133.8	3196.2	10575.0
	M	719.3	1271.3	112.2	43.1	112.3	132.4	277.5	562.0	1496.0	4104.0	11999.8
	F	588.4	984.3	84.0	27.5	51.8	78.3	149.6	339.5	832.2	2432.3	9663.3
Philippines	T	704.8	7007.6	949.3	157.5	163.5	232.6	422.3	713.9	1260.4	5429.5	
	M	791.9	7777.2	984.9	172.5	206.2	281.4	493.3	903.7	1586.8	5670.7	
	F	618.5	6163.5	911.9	141.7	123.6	186.1	349.6	540.5	968.9	5200.3	
Thailand	T	534.7	2182.0	468.8	159.9	235.1	311.2	477.0	914.8	1671.7	3438.6	9389.5
	M	716.5	2469.6	485.7	172.1	290.0	380.3	555.1	1113.5	2074.7	4268.4	11014.7
	F	553.8	1875.9	451.5	147.3	182.6	245.1	399.0	720.0	1290.3	2746.5	8319.0
Colombia	T	713.1	5824.8	748.1	129.3	187.8	254.2	394.7	711.9	1663.4	4204.4	8965.3
	M	767.6	6343.1	728.2	141.1	235.8	312.0	425.8	785.4	1881.6	4690.6	9266.3
	F	660.2	5290.7	758.2	117.3	144.7	201.4	364.9	638.9	1451.6	3765.9	8737.9
Mexico	T	845.1	5185.3	723.7	125.6	213.4	345.3	543.2	904.6	1697.3	3721.6	10098.0
	M	917.3	5684.8	713.7	135.5	266.5	424.8	651.8	1080.3	1927.7	4010.0	10001.0
	F	773.1	4667.9	734.1	115.3	163.1	269.3	437.2	727.3	1473.1	3441.2	10178.5
Peru	T	640.3	7237.8	744.1	93.0	133.3	196.2	323.1	488.2	999.5	2363.5	9109.2
	M	656.2	7639.2	730.9	97.3	131.4	191.0	324.6	543.2	1147.3	2662.6	9080.3
	F	624.3	6816.3	757.8	88.6	135.1	201.6	321.6	433.7	859.6	2097.0	9132.1

SOURCE: United Nations (1976e:Table 7).

Table 23B. Death Rates Specific for Sex and Age, Per 100,000 Population (Infant Deaths Per 100,000 Live-Born) (Euro-North America)

Country	Sex	All Ages	0	1-4	5-14	15-24	25-34	35-44	45-54	55-64	65-74	75+
France	T	1055.7	1262.5	74.5	36.3	106.9	115.8	253.2	577.7	1344.0	3069.2	9867.7
	M	1110.2	1409.4	83.1	43.1	151.7	156.8	338.6	801.2	1939.9	4351.8	11880.1
	F	1003.4	1107.6	65.6	29.3	60.0	71.1	163.8	360.4	820.0	2103.5	8932.7
Hungary	T	1182.6	3383.6	84.5	34.2	83.3	130.5	274.4	627.6	1602.9	4079.5	12074.7
	M	1267.0	3823.6	95.9	41.7	119.3	178.6	364.1	812.5	2083.8	5176.1	13898.7
	F	1103.0	2914.0	72.4	26.2	45.5	82.0	189.4	461.1	1196.2	3233.5	11025.0
Sweden	T	1057.6	950.2	43.9	27.9	68.6	90.5	181.5	451.2	1077.7	2879.9	9870.9
	M	1170.2	1049.7	49.0	32.2	95.2	124.0	231.8	585.2	1429.1	3760.8	11653.3
	F	946.0	844.5	38.5	23.4	40.9	54.7	129.8	317.6	736.7	2125.5	8653.6
Spain	T	856.8	1520.6	90.9	38.8	75.1	106.5	201.9	483.5	1214.1	3292.7	10888.3
	M	905.1	1724.8	97.1	46.6	104.4	139.4	260.3	638.4	1654.3	4271.3	12002.0
	F	810.7	1304.2	84.3	30.5	45.4	73.9	145.3	337.7	846.8	2546.0	10217.1
United Kingdom	T	1194.7	1687.5	69.0	30.5	69.4	79.5	190.4	578.2	1506.6	3735.6	11208.9
	M	1240.0	1892.6	77.0	37.0	95.7	100.7	225.0	723.1	2042.2	5151.4	13635.7
	F	1151.8	1469.1	60.5	23.6	42.1	57.9	155.2	437.2	1022.2	2684.8	10098.3
United States	T	940.2	1771.8	79.5	41.0	128.2	153.6	295.9	697.4	1611.9	3440.0	9841.4
	M	1072.8	1988.8	88.8	50.0	189.8	214.5	380.4	916.6	2206.6	4731.5	11841.1
	F	814.1	1543.5	69.9	31.6	66.4	94.4	215.6	493.1	1079.8	2445.5	8635.9

SOURCE: United Nations (1976e:Table 7).

The incidence of hypothermia among people over sixty-five admitted to a group of hospitals in London was three times as high in 1975 as is 1966, according to a survey published in London by the Royal College of Physicians.

The continuing seriousness of hypothermia has been described by Hugh Faulkner, Hon. Director of Help the Aged, as "one of the scandals of our time."

He said the figures showed that as many as 81,000 more old people die in Britain during winter months than during the summer.

More than two million old people live in temperatures which are so low that they could bring prosecution if occuring in factories or offices (from *Help Age International* May 1977:16).

Nursing homes and homes for the elderly tend to be sources of scandal in many countries regardless of material wealth. The removal of autonomy of decision-making from the elderly about the care of their own persons frequently puts them in the hands of persons who misdiagnose their condition and thus further limit their freedom through inappropriate hospitalization or actual confinement in mental institutions. A study at New York City's Bellevue hospital revealed that of 116 patients over sixty-five admitted to the hospitals psychiatric ward, seventy-one had treatable physical ailments rather than psychological disorders (Reported in *Help Age International* March 1977:3).

The need for retirement clinics set up to serve the elderly as children's clinics are set up to serve the special medical needs of the young is great, yet discussions are just beginning about the desirability of such clinics. Day care centers for the elderly that provide for many of the physical and social needs without depriving them of their own home are beginning to spread in Europe and the United States. Stockholm has set up a very successful program of opening school lunch rooms to the elderly, so that any Stockholm pensioner over sixty-five is welcome to lunch at any of the tewnty-three schools in the city. Menus for all school meals are published in advance in the newspapers, so pensioners can take their pick of meals offered at the various schools. Hospices, an English invention are also spreading. These are centers where the dying can spend their last days in dignity and full awareness of the important work of closing a life, instead of being hidden feafully in the anonymity of a hospital ward.

An added source of misery at the two ends of the age spectrum are the practices of child abuse and grandparent abuse. Poorly reported but received growing attention and concern in the industrial countries, these acts of deliberately inflicting injury on the young and the old are in a sense the answer of the proportionately shrinking population in the middle third of life to the concentration of responsibility thrust upon them. It is found in homes where middle-years parents are caught between the pressures of childrearing and the care of elderly parents. If the elderly were themselves abusive to their children when they were young, the chances of being in turn abused are greatly increased. But even with no abuse history, the pressures of family life may drive young parents to batter their elders. Outright beating is perhaps less common than pushing and shoving and shaking that results in falls and injuries that may require hospitalization. Other devices are tying them down in chairs, locking them in rooms, or putting them out on the street with orders not to come back for a stated number of hours, or outright abandonment on a deserted street. The total dependence of these elderly on their adult children, and their lack of alternatives, perceived or real, drives them to minimize their own suffering. Parents of all ages probably always rate their relationships with their children higher than children rate their relationship with their parents, and so even the battered elderly manage to redefine their situation so it is "not so bad." Like many battered children, they will defend their abusers to neighbors and public officials.

On the positive side, efforts like the "adopt a grandparent" movement, which has spread rapidly across the United States in the 1970s, represents a positive reaching out to reintegrate the elderly into the very communities that have been rejecting them. The concept involves a two-way relationship of mutual friendships, respect and aid. It provides children with needed wise elders and elders with needed young companionship.

From a policy perspective, much more public health and welfare infrastructure will be required to ease the current strain on elder-middle years relationships. Even the most industrialized societies, with high aspirations for a good life for all, wear blinders in regard to the aged. Welfare programs for senior citizens are usually linked to pre-retirement income, thus not simply perpetuating previous poverty for the elderly poor, but sharply increasing it at the very time when extra resources are needed to keep warm enough, well fed enough, well enough. Of the eight countries whose community services for senior citizens are described in Table 25, only one, the United Kingdom, does not link retirement aid to previous income.

In the United States, a recent report uncovers systematic failure to make welfare programs available to the elderly and to children:

> A 15-month study conducted by the U.S. Commission on Civil Rights, inquiring into 10 federally financed programs that are mainly administered by State and local authorities, has concluded

Table 24A. Death Rates Specific for Sex and Age, Per 100,000 Population, from suicide and Self-Inflicted Injury (Asia and Latin America)

Country	Sex	All Ages	0	1-4	5-14	15-24	25-34	35-44	45-54	55-64	65-74	75+
Japan	T	17.3	—	—	0.6	16.5	18.0	17.4	18.5	28.0	48.8	79.0
	M	20.1	—	—	0.8	19.9	22.4	22.9	21.7	33.6	53.5	87.4
	F	14.7	—	—	0.3	13.1	13.7	11.8	15.7	23.3	44.9	73.7
Philippines	T	1.4	—	—	0.1	3.3	2.0	1.4	1.7	1.7		2.1
	M	1.6	—	—	0.1	3.6	2.4	1.9	2.7	3.0		3.4
	F	1.1	—	—	0.2	3.1	1.6	1.0	0.9	0.6		0.8
Thailand	T	4.4	—	—	0.5	10.5	6.3	5.6	5.6	5.1	5.3	6.4
	M	4.9	—	—	0.4	9.6	7.6	7.4	8.5	7.8	7.8	12.5
	F	3.9	—	—	0.7	11.5	5.0	3.9	2.7	2.5	3.2	2.4
Colombia	T	3.5	—	—	0.4	7.6	6.2	4.9	5.3	4.7	6.4	5.0
	M	4.9	—	—	0.4	8.6	10.7	8.0	8.4	8.7	13.1	9.7
	F	2.1	—	—	0.4	6.8	2.2	1.9	2.2	0.9	0.4	1.5
Mexico	T	0.7	—	—	—	1.3	1.2	1.2	1.2	1.4	1.7	1.6
	M	1.1	—	—	—	1.9	1.8	2.2	1.9	2.5	3.3	2.9
	F	0.3	—	—	—	0.7	0.5	0.3	0.4	0.3	0.1	0.5
Peru	T	1.8	—	—	—	3.5	2.7	2.5	3.2	2.5	4.1	7.4
	M	2.4	—	—	—	3.5	3.7	4.1	5.8	4.5	8.1	8.4
	F	1.2	—	—	—	3.6	1.7	0.9	0.6	0.7	0.6	6.6

SOURCE: United Nations (1976e:Table 7).

Table 24B. Death Rates Specific for Sex and Age, Per 100,000 Population, from Suicide and Self-Inflicted Injury (Euro-North America)

Country	Sex	All Ages	0	1-4	5-14	15-24	25-34	35-44	45-54	55-64	65-74	75+
France	T	15.5	—	—	0.3	7.7	12.1	16.6	23.8	30.5	35.1	39.4
	M	22.6	—	—	0.5	11.0	17.1	25.1	35.4	45.3	55.9	83.0
	F	8.7	—	—	0.1	4.3	6.7	7.7	12.5	17.6	19.4	19.1
Hungary	T	36.9	—	—	1.1	15.7	31.8	40.2	55.2	62.0	76.2	109.0
	M	53.2	—	—	1.9	24.8	48.7	64.4	82.7	92.5	106.0	177.4
	F	21.5	—	—	0.3	6.1	14.8	17.3	30.4	36.2	53.2	69.6
Sweden	T	20.1	—	—	0.3	12.5	21.1	26.4	32.9	31.5	31.8	24.2
	M	28.7	—	—	0.5	17.2	31.3	37.0	47.6	40.0	49.1	47.4
	F	11.5	—	—	—	7.5	10.3	15.4	18.3	23.2	17.0	8.3
Spain	T	4.2	—	—	0.2	1.4	2.7	4.2	6.8	9.3	13.6	14.1
	M	6.2	—	—	0.3	1.9	4.1	6.1	9.8	14.1	23.2	27.0
	F	2.3	—	—	0.0	0.8	1.3	2.3	4.0	5.2	6.3	6.4
United Kingdom	T	7.8	—	—	0.1	4.4	7.2	10.2	12.0	13.3	14.6	14.2
	M	9.4	—	—	0.1	5.7	9.8	12.7	13.6	16.3	18.8	22.1
	F	6.2	—	—	0.1	3.0	4.6	7.7	10.5	10.7	11.5	10.6
United States	T	12.0	—	—	0.4	10.6	14.9	16.4	19.5	20.3	19.8	21.1
	M	17.7	—	—	0.6	17.0	21.9	21.8	26.9	30.5	34.5	44.7
	F	6.5	—	—	0.2	4.3	8.1	11.3	12.6	11.2	8.5	6.8

SOURCE: United Nations (1976e:Table 7).

that many children and older persons are being denied access to federal services and benefits solely because of their age, with the elderly receiving the bulk of the rejections. The commission declares itself "shocked at the cavalier manner in which our society neglects older persons who often desperately need federally-supported services and benefits." The Commission notes that many administrators of federally financed programs feel they get a "better return" on the government's investment by helping young adults, especially in the areas of health care, rehabilitation, and job training . . . (From *Behavior Today* January 23, 1967)

Civic Participation of the Young and the Old

Because survival into the older years of substantial numbers of people is a new phenomenon in this century, movements for civic participation of the elderly in public affairs and in shaping the conditions of their own lives are fairly recent. Table 26 shows how recent the development of transnational nongovernmental organization networks (NGO's) for the elderly has been. The oldest organization was founded in 1950. By contrast, youth and those concerned with youth have been developing transnational networks since the 1890s. The reader may compare this data with the data on children and youth related NGOs in Tables 7A through 7E. In contrast to the six organizations for and about the elderly, there are 103 for and about children and youth. The largest organization for the elderly has sections in only twenty-two countries, where the largest youth NGO has sections in 115 countries. NGOs are least accessible to third world young and old, since such organizations depend on urban-based networks.

NGOs represent the privileged elite of both youth and age. At the same time they have a grassroots potential, in that every national section represents the possibility of widespread local organization within a country. At the local level, each country is developing its own participatory patterns for newly aroused senior citizens. The Grey Panthers is a highly successful political activist group for senior citizens in the United States, and its counterparts are developing in other countries, kept in touch by the international newspaper for the elderly, *Help Age International*. In France the Grandmères Bénvoles has recently organized to help young mothers with child care. The adopt-a-grandparent movement in the United States has taken a new turn with senior citizens coming into the public schools as tutors. As the number of senior citizens grows in each country, we can expect more new associations and projects initiated by them. We can also expect more activity of senior citizens in the main body of civic and service associations of every kind. The models are ther — a few highly visible dynamic elderly who entered the public arena on the wave of nineteenth century internationalism and kept active in their eighties and nineties, like John Boyd Orr of the World Health organization, and Rebecca Shelley of the Women's International League for Peace and Freedom. If the "adopt-a-grandparent" movement is any indicator, we can also expect new associations which join the young and the old. Necessary as all these developments are they stem from the middle classes, and leave the plight of the poor elderly untouched. They remain as a challenge to the social imagination of all ages.

THE REINCORPORATION OF THE AWARE CHILD AND THE WISE ELDER INTO SOCIETY

We have examined how gender and age interact to limit the participation of women, and of the young and the old, in ways that do not relate to individual capabilities. We have noted that these limitations are varied in extent and effect according to degree of industrialization, and according to family-transmitted social class. The model presented at the beginning of Part III conceptualizes a series of sorting processes, beginning with the level of industrialization of a society and going on to the family socioeconomic status, each of which in turn determine life chances of an individual before birth. At birth gender provides a further sorting process, ensuring greater longevity for females but a wider range of life chances for males. Pronounced gender sorting does not begin until puberty, and from puberty on women and men move through similar age sorting but with far greater role shifts for women than for men. Age sorting into adult hood does not occur until some years after entry into laborforce/marriage/childbearing status, causing great role strain in this period.

If age sorting into adulthood is excessively postponed, age sorting into retirement and the status of being elderly is excessively premature. The age sorting process mismatches responsibility, status and capacity from puberty on, particularly in industrial societies. This mismatch puts a heavy loading on the middle third of life as the only period in which persons participate fully in the work of maintaining and shaping society and their own lives. It also puts a special kind of loading on women who carry extra responsibilities without full civic status. As the world moves toward population equilibrium with declining resouces, an aging society will need the fuller participation and wisdom of its elders, as well as the awareness, inventiveness, and energy of its young. Removal of legal age barriers to full civic status will be required. This means a reconsideration

Table 25. Community Services for the Elderly in Eight Countries

Country	Old age and Retirement Pension		Health Care		Long term Care Facilities	Home Helps
	Type	Coverage	Type	Coverage	(1)	(2)
Canada	Flat grant Wage-related Income tested	Universal	Hospital and Medical Insurance	Almost universal	9	*
France	Wage-related	77% and others in special programmes	Cash benefits and Health Insurance	"	5	1:7,000
	Income tested (also some special cash benefits) Mandatory private pensions					
FRG	Wage-related	84% and others in special programmes	Health Insurance	"	5	1:6,000
	Income tested					

Table 25 (cont'd)

Country	Old age and Retirement Pension				Long term Care Facilities (1)	Home Helps (2)
	Type	Coverage	Type	Coverage		
Israel	Wage-related Income tested	Almost universal	Voluntary Health Insurance	85-90% partial coverage	*	*
Poland	Wage-related Income tested	75%	Health services	100%	1+	Very limited
UK	Flat grant Wage related Income tested	Almost universal	"	"	3	1:700
USA	Wage-related	Almost universal	Medical and Hospital Insurance	Partial coverage for aged 65+ Supplementary coverage income tested	5	1:7,000
Yugoslavia	Very little coverage and benefit levels in all programmes				0.4	Very limited

1. Percentage of the elderly covered by long-term care facilities.
2. Ratio of home-helps to the aged.

Source: Table reproduced from Help Age International, March 1977:9, based on a study by Sheila Kamerman of Columbia University, U.S.A.

Table 26. NGOs For and About the Elderly

Name	Purpose	Number of National Sections	Year Founded
ECGDR*	Research	5, W. Europe	1964
EFWE*	Int'l cooperation in welfare projects by the elderly	W. Europe, no number reported	1962
IAG*	Research	33, N. and S. America, E. and W. Europe, Asia	1950
ICHHS*	Service, including to elderly	18, N. America, Asia, W. Europe	1959
ISCA*	Forum for senior citizens, cultural, educational	16, N. America, Africa, Asia, W. Europe	1963
ICSG*	Research and action	22	1969

*ECGDR = European Centre for Gerontological Documentation and Research
 EFWE = European Federation for the Welfare of the Elderly
 IAG   = International Association of Gerontology
 ICHHS = International Council of Home-Help Services
 ISCA = International Senior Citizens Association, Inc.
 ICSG = International Center of Social Gerontology

SOURCE: Yearbook of International Organizations (1974).

of the issue of whether or not *age* is a constitutionally suspect category in the laws of nation states, and of whether or not *age* is an unlawful basis of discrimination in the United Nations Declaration of Human Rights. For more and less industrialized societies alike it means a careful examination of development policy in terms of education and employment infrastructures, and of the implicit or explicit age grading policies associated with these infrastructures.

The life cycle perspective offered in this study, buttressed with statistics about actual participation rates of human beings in various age categories and by gender, makes clear the inequalities of age sorting. In terms of the ideal of a heterostatic society engaged in a continuous process of complex balancing of human capacities, needs and resources, as discussed earlier, the rigidities of age sorting are clearly counterproductive. The same life-cycle perspective, by demonstrating the gradual growth from undifferentiated to differentiated androgyny, suggests alternatives to ancient customs of gender sorting in the years between puberty and menopause. Such alternatives might foster more differentiated personality development in both sexes, and produce a more peaceful and humanly fulfilling social order.

The concept of the wise elder needs to be rediscovered. As long as so many economic and legal constraints prevent the senior citizen from coming into full flowering, a vicious cycle of social impoverishment is fostered. Because the elderly seem like a burden to the middle-years folk, they restrict their life space even further, making the elderly in turn even more dependent and ill. The release of the senior citizen "back in" to society will in contrast initiate a benevolent cycle. The seniors will be enabled to be more self-sufficient, will in the process become more healthy (taking responsibility for one's own life is a well-recognized step toward recovering from illness) and will be able to take on a range of community roles as well as contribute to the economic life of their society. The aware, inventive child also needs to be rediscovered. Children and youth can take more responsibility for their own lives, and contribute more to the common welfare, than society allows them to. Collaboration with the elderly and the young in the economic and civic spheres, and recovery of relationships with those excluded members of society, will take a great physical burden from middle-years adults. Most important of all, it will release them from a great burden of guilt. Instead of having to deny to themselves that they were ever children, or will ever be old, they will be able to rediscover their own wholeness. They will find their own inner child-person, and their own inner elder-to-be. This liberation of middle-years adults will release the pressure on children and youth, and create the conditions for a kind of intergenerational partnership we do not now have.

Most important, the rediscovery of the wise elder and the child opens up the possibility of drawing on a wider range of human experience for social problem solving. It will generate more new learning for each generation, and make possible more new combinations of thought, new action inventions for the future.

It was originally intended to draw up a Declaration of the Rights of the Elderly for this Section. On further reflection, the simple statement that human rights should not begin at a certain age or end at a certain age seems more to the point. There was reason to spell out details about human rights for children because there are so many misconceptions about the capabilities of the young. At the extreme ends of the lifespan, for the very young and the very old, there are physiological reasons why "protection rights" need to be available. How this can be handled in terms of need without creating categories that deprive capable persons of their autonomy, and without destroying the achievements of a legal system that has moved well beyond ad hoc law, has still to be worked out. It is not clear how society will move in the future in the matter of enhancing opportunity and individuality for each human being. The device of class action suits for giving equal rights to various categories of human beings has been very important in the recent past. How can we use classificatory concepts without destroying the personhood of human beings? At the very least, a rethinking of the social category of age and the acceptance of the aware child and the wise elder into our midst is a possible next step as we move into the twenty-first century. We must not continue to waste our very substance as we face problems too big for any generation to handle alone. Nor should we perpetuate old cycles by forgetting how it felt to be set aside as a child, and by failing to remember that we ourselves will one day feel as the old now feel. We need not be trapped by the past, if we will recognize and affirm the wheel of life, on which we all turn, and through which we find our wholeness as members of the human species.

NOTES

1. Various kinds of "Living together" arrangements without marriage are not considered in the model, for simplicity's sake, though they may affect status of both men and women.
2. It has been pointed out to me that children's activities in tribal societies are also strongly sex-stereotyped, since little girls are expected to stay close to home and help their mothers. Perhaps I should modify the statement to say that what freedom girl children have, they use in freer ways before puberty in any society.
3. Lowenthal et al.s (1976) study of four major life transitions: (1) leaving home, (2) starting a family, (3) the empty nest and (4) retirement, for a group of middle and lower class white Americans corroborates much that has been said both about stress points in the life cycle and about later-life androgyny. Women who have been greatly stressed in earlier stages blossom at retirement age. Men, less stressed at earlier stages, generally do less well with the role transformation at retirement. Those that do well take on a more nurturant style. Maas and Kuypers' (1975) study of life history data going back to age thirty of women and men now in their seventies similarly emphasize differences in adaptive styles of women and men at different stages of the life cycle, and find that women are more responsive than men to changing contexts in old age. The style of aging of husband and wife in old age appear to be quite independent, each of the other.
4. Twenty-one to twenty-five is an anomalous age status, with full legal rights for men, but not yet full recognition of civic adulthood.
5. A sympathetic journalist quotes a letter from an unhappy sixty-year-old woman in the November-December 1977 issue of the London-published newspaper, *Help Age International:*
    . . . I am haunted by the fear that if I cannot dispel the assumption that I am a senior-citizen, the following events will occur: I shall have a gang of young thugs sent to my home to paint my kitchen instead of going to

prison; I shall have patients from the local mental hospital drafted to dig my garden; I may be forced to go to suitable entertainments, drink tea and wear a paper hat . . . We pensioners are in a terrifying position. We are recipients . . . hands off, please. I am in charge of my life.

6. Much of what is labelled withdrawal is in fact the byproduct of structural arrangements of a neighborhood and location of kin and friends. Rosenberg's (1970) study of elderly working class women and men indicates that in the absence of structural barriers the elderly may develop friendship in their own neighborhoods with those who are both older and younger than themselves, and are not necessarily isolates at all. On the other hand it cannot be overlooked that large numbers of elderly people are very lonely indeed. See the report by *Help Age International,* "Cry and You Cry Alone" (1978).

7. It is a well-known phenomenon in the international women's peace movement that women in their nineties are more forward-looking and optimistic than their younger colleagues.

8. In our conceptual model the age breaks are under twenty-four, twenty-five to fifty-five, and over fifty-five. In order to emphasize the employment situation at the extremes of youth and age, however, the discussion that follows emphasizes the under-nineteens and the over sixty-fives.

9. Divorce figures for the elderly are not included in Table 22 because not enough countries report these figures.

10. There is no one set pattern for such "universities." The term represents an umbrella concept including everything from university-type courses offered in special extension settings to hobby-type adult education programs. One concern of people working with such "universities" is to upgrade the quality of the more hobby-type courses and to develop and maintain a common standard.

11. This analysis is based on World Health Organization causes of death statistics (United Nations 1976e). While suicide statistics may be questioned, reporting is steadily improving. Differences within and between countries appear consistent with other data, though reported absolute levels may in some countries be unrealistically low.

12. The following note from a sociologist teaching and doing community work in Zambia throws some light on the difficulty of making meaningful statements on this subject:

    Considering suicide rates in the first and third world, I seem to hear about many more suicides both in Zambia and Sri Lanka than I ever did in Norway. I think at least you should modify your statement about higher first world rates, by pointing to the very poor statistics that exist in most third world countries. Otherwise you seem to convey the image of the "happy native" — and that non-whites do not feel like whites over personal adversities, losses of off-spring etc. (Else Skjonsberg, Chipata, Zambia).

Appendix A

DECLARATION OF THE RIGHTS OF THE CHILD

Preamble

Whereas the people of the United Nations have, in the Charter, reaffirmed their faith in fundamental human rights, and in the dignity and worth of the human person, and have determined to promote social progress and better standards of life in larger freedom,

Whereas the United Nations has, in the Universal Declaration of Human Rights, proclaimed that everyone is entitled to all the rights and freedoms set forth therein, without distinction of any kind, such as race, color, sex, language, religion, political or other opinion, national or social origin, property, birth or other status,

Whereas the child, by reason of his physical and mental immaturity, needs special safeguards and care, including appropriate legal protection before as well as after birth,

Whereas the need for such special safeguards has been stated in the Geneva Declaration of the Rights of the Child of 1924, and recognized in the Universal Declaration of Human Rights and in the statutes of specialized agencies and international organizations concerned with the welfare of children,

Whereas mankind owes to the child the best it has to give,

Now therefore,

The General Assembly

Proclaims this Declaration of the Rights of the Child to the end that he may have a happy childhood and enjoy for his own good and for the good of society the rights and freedoms herein set forth, and calls upon parents, upon men and women as individuals and upon voluntary organizations, local authorities and national governments to recognize these rights and strive for their observance by legislative and other measures progressively taken in accordance with the following principles:

Principle 1

The child shall enjoy all the rights set forth in this Declaration. All children, without any exception whatsoever, shall be entitled to these rights, without distinction or discrimination on account of race, color, sex, language, religion, political or other opinion, national or social origin, property, birth or other status, whether of himself or of his family.

Principle 2

The child shall enjoy special protection, and shall be given opportunities and facilities, by law and by other means, to enable him to develop physically, mentally, morally, spiritually and socially in a healthy and normal manner and in conditions of freedom and dignity. In the enactment of laws for this purpose the best interests of the child shall be the paramount consideration.

Principle 3

The child shall be entitled from his birth to a name and a nationality.

Principle 4

The child shall enjoy the benefits of social security. He shall be entitled to grow and develop in heath; to this end special care and protection shall be provided both to him and to his mother, including adequate pre-natal and post-natal care. The child shall have the right to adequate nutrition, housing recreation and medical services.

Principle 5

The child who is physically, mentally or socially handicapped shall be given the special treatment, education and care required by his particular condition.

Principle 6

The child, for the full and harmonious development of his personality, needs love and understanding. He shall, wherever possible, grow up in the care and under the responsibility of his parents, and in any case in an atmosphere of affection and of moral and material security; a child of tender years shall not, save in exceptional circumstances, be separated from his mother. Society and the public authorities shall have the duty to extend particular care to children without a family and to those without adequate means of support. Payment of state and other assistance toward the maintenance of children of large families is desirable.

Principle 7

The child is entitled to receive education, which shall be free and compulsory, at least in the elementary stages. He shall be given an education which will promote his general culture, and enable him on a basis of equal opportunity to develop his abilities, his individual judgment, and his sense of moral and social responsibility, and to become a useful member of society.

The best interests of the child shall be the guiding principle of those responsible for his education and guidance; that responsibility lies in the first place with his parents.

The child shall have full opportunity for play and recreation, which should be directed to the same purposes as education; society and the public authorities shall endeavor to promote the enjoyment of this right.

Principle 8

The child shall in all circumstances be among the first to receive protection and relief.

Principle 9

The child shall be protected against all forms of neglect, cruelty and exploitation. He shall not be the subject of traffic, in any form.

The child shall not be admitted to employment before an appropriate minimum age; he shall in no case be caused or permitted to engage in any occupation or employment which would prejudice his health or education, or interfere with his physical, mental or moral development.

Principle 10

The child shall be protected from practices which may foster racial, religious and any other form of discrimination. He shall be brought up in a spirit of understanding, tolerance, friendship among people, peace and universal brotherhood and in full consciousness that his energy and talents should be devoted to the service of his fellow men.

> Untied Nations, General Assembly Resolution 1386(XIV), November 20, 1959, published in the *Official Records of the General Assembly, Fourteenth Session, Supplement No. 16, 1960, p.19. Source: Wilkerson (1973:3-6).*

WHY NOT A BILL OF RIGHTS FOR CHILDREN? (from Holt, 1974).

1. The right to equal treatment at the hands of the law — i.e., the right, in any situation, to be treated no worse than an adult would be.
2. The right to vote and take full part in political affairs.
3. The right to be legally responsible for one's life and acts.
4. The right to work, for money.
5. The right to privacy.
6. The right to financial independence and responsibility — i.e., the right to own, buy, and sell property, to borrow money, establish credit, sign contracts, etc.
7. The right to direct and manage one's own education.
8. The right to travel, to live away from home, to choose or make one's own home.
9. The right to receive from the state whatever minimum income it may guarantee to adult citizens.
10. The right to make and enter into, on a basis of mutual consent, quasi-familial relationships outside one's immediate family — i.e., the right to seek and choose guardians other than one's own parents and to be legally dependent on them.
11. The right to do, in general, what any adult may legally do.

A CHILD'S BILL OF RIGHTS (from Farson, 1974).

1. THE RIGHT TO SELF-DETERMINATION. *Children should have the right to decide the matters that affect them most directly.* This is the basic right upon which all others depend. Children are now treated as the private property of their parents on the assumption that it is the parents' right and responsibility to control the life of the child. The achievement of children's right, however, would reduce the need for this control and bring about an end to the double standard of morals and behavior for adults and children.

2. THE RIGHT TO ALTERNATE HOME ENVIRONMENTS. *Self-determining children should be able to choose from among a variety of arrangements: residences operated by children, child-exchange programs, twenty-four-hour child-care centers, and various kinds of schools and employment opportunities.* Parents are not always good for their children — some people estimate that as many as 4 million children are abused annually in the United States, for instance, and that a half million children run away each year.

3. THE RIGHT TO RESPONSIVE DESIGN. *Society must accommodate itself to children's size and to their need for safe space.* To keep them in their place, we now force children to cope with a world that is either not built to fit them or is actually designed against them. If the environment were less dangerous for children, there would be less need for constant control and supervision of children by adults.

4. THE RIGHT TO INFORMATION. *A child must have the right to all information ordinarily available to adults — including, and perhaps especially, information that makes adults uncomfortable.*

5. THE RIGHT TO EDUCATE ONESELF. *Children should be free to design their own education, choosing from among many options the kinds of learning experiences they want, including the option not to attend any kind of school.* Compulsory education must be abolished, because the enforced, threatening quality of education in America has taught children to hate school, to hate the subject matter, and, tragically, to hate themselves. Children are programmed, tracked, and certified in a process of stamping out standardized educated products acceptable to the university, military, business and industry, and community. Education can change only through the achievement of new rights for those exploited and oppressed by it — the children themselves.

6.   THE RIGHT TO FREEDOM FROM PHYSICAL PUNISHMENT. *Children should live free of physical threat from those who are larger and more powerful than they.* Corporal punishment is used impulsively and cruelly in the home, arbitrarily in the school, and sadistically in penal institutions. It does not belong in our repertoire of responses to children.

7. THE RIGHT TO SEXUAL FREEDOM. *Children should have the right to conduct their sexual lives with no more restriction than adults.* Sexual freedom for children must include the right to information about sex, the right to non-sexist education, and the right to all sexual activities that are legal among consenting adults. In fact, children will be best protected from sexual abuse when they have the right to refuse — but they are now trained *not* to refuse adults, to accept all forms of physical affection, and to mistrust their own reactions to people. They are denied any information about their own sexuality or that of others. We keep them innocent and ignorant and then worry that they will not be able to resist sexual approaches.

8. THE RIGHT TO ECONOMIC POWER. *Children should have the right to work, to acquire and manage money, to receive equal pay for equal work, to choose trade apprenticeship as an alternative to school, to gain promotion to leadership positions, to own property, to develop a credit record, to enter into binding contracts, to engage in enterprise, to obtain guaranteed support apart from the family, to achieve financial independence.*

9. THE RIGHT TO POLITICAL POWER. *Children should have the vote and be included in the decision-making process.* Eighty million children in the United States need the right to vote, because adults do not vote in their behalf. At present they are no one's constituency, and legislation reflects that lack of representation. To become a constituency, they must have the right to vote.

10. THE RIGHT TO JUSTICE. *Children must have the guarantee of a fair trial with due process of law, an advocate to protect their rights against the parents as well as the system, and a uniform standard of detention.* Every year, a million children get into trouble with the law. One out of every nine children will go through the juvenile court system before the age of eighteen.

YOUTH LIBERATION PROGRAM:
YOUTH LIBERATION OF ANN ARBOR

Every day, it becomes clearer that we might be the last generation in the experiment with living. The problems facing humanity are so huge that some of us think working for change is futile. We of Youth Liberation, however, will not be led either to the treadmill or to the slaughterhouse like "good Germans." We know there is a basic decision to make: either we stay quiet and become part of a system of oppression, or we seize control of our lives, take risks, and struggle to build something new. We believe that problems have causes and that by studying these causes we can learn solutions. We know that young people have power if we take it and use it. We must liberate ourselves from the death trip of corporate America. We must take control of our lives, because within us is the seed of a new reality — a seed that cannot grow until our lives are our own. It is a reality of ecstasy, made up of love, justice, freedom, peace, and plenty.

The Youth Liberation Program is an attempt to put together truth about what is wrong with our present situation and to lay out changes that must be made. This process never ends. To win, we must know very clearly what we want and what we reject. We are learning to struggle together. If our program strays from the specific needs of youth, it is because we know that we are not free until all people are free and the earth is a healthy place to live.

1. WE WANT THE POWER TO DETERMINE OUR OWN DESTINY.

2. WE WANT THE IMMEDIATE END OF ADULT CHAUVINISM. We believe ideas should be judged on their merit and people on their wisdom or kindness. Age in itself deserves no recognition. Adults who want to support youth struggle or "improve communication" should show their conern by providing concrete resources. Words alone are not enough. Age might once have led to wisdom, but the old have proved themselves unable to deal with present reality. If the human species is to survive, the young must take the lead.

3. WE WANT FULL CIVIL AND HUMAN RIGHTS. We believe young people are necessary participants in democracy. We must have complete freedom of speech, press, assembly, and religion, and the right to vote. We believe that all people are created equal and are endowed with certain unalienable rights; among these are life, liberty and the pursuit of happiness.

4. WE WANT THE RIGHT TO FORM OUR EDUCATION ACCORDING TO OUR NEEDS. We believe compulsory education is a form of imprisonment and must be abolished immediately. Grades and all forms of tracking must end, because they stimulate competition, divide us, and make us work for other people's ends. All discipline procedures must be decided democratically within the school community. No school staff should be hired or fired without the democratic consent of students and teachers. Students and the community must have the right to use school facilities whenever they feel it is necessary.

5. WE WANT THE FREEDOM TO FORM INTO COMMUNAL FAMILIES. We believe that the nuclear family is not in the best interest of the people involved. Young people are now considered property — to be molded in the image of their parents. Since we demand self-determination for our lives, this is intolerable. In communal families children can grow in the company of many people, both peers and adults. They can learn the cooperation of community rather than the oppression of ownership. Until communal families are a reality, some healthy provision must be made for young people whose present conditions of life force them to become cultural refugees.

6. WE WANT THE END OF MALE CHAUVINISM AND SEXISM. We believe women must be free and equal. We recognize that sexism is all-pervasive and often subtle and demeans the humanity of everyone. All forms of sex-role stereotyping must end. Macho must go. Abortions must be free

and legal. We consider the women's movement our natural ally since both young people and women are systematically oppressed by male-supremacist society.

7. WE WANT THE OPPORTUNITY TO CREATE AN AUTHENTIC CULTURE WITH INSTITUTIONS OF OUR OWN MAKING. We believe western culture is decadent and we refuse to continue it in our lives. People's appearance must not affect their civil rights. All drugs must be legalized, as we see that it is not laws that govern people's use of drugs, but societal conditions. We hope to create a society in which people will not need death drugs. Our music and cultural gatherings must be allowed to flourish in peace. We must be set free to begin living in the new age and begin to accept a responsibility for developing plans and examples of institutions that build joy, justice, and a respect for life.

8. WE WANT SEXUAL SELF-DETERMINATION. We believe all people must have the unhindered right to be heterosexual, homosexual, bisexual, or transsexual.

9. WE WANT THE END OF CLASS ANTAGONISM AMONG YOUNG PEOPLE. We believe that those in power cultivate elitism and class divisions among youth which only serve to weaken us. The survival of young people of all classes and races is threatened by the few who run this world. We condemn academic tracking, honors, and all other class divisions imposed upon us.

10. WE WANT THE END OF RACISIM AND COLONIALISM IN THE UNITED STATES AND THE WORLD. We believe America is an imperialist country. America uses over 50 percent of the world's resources for less than 7 percent of the world's population. Racism in schools is severly damaging to students, particularly minority students. Students must eliminate racism and stop fighting each other. We must unite to fight the real enemy until we have education that meets the needs of all races. We support the liberation struggles of colonized people of all colors everywhere.

11. WE WANT FREEDOM FOR ALL UNJUSTLY IMPRISONED PEOPLE. All young people in juvenile homes, training schools, detention centers, mental institutions and other penal institutions for minors must be set free. They did not receive a trial before a jury of their peers, and the society they offended is itself criminal. Young people must never receive discriminatory treatment before the law, whether in the courtroom, going to a movie, buying alcohol, leaving home. The military draft must be abolished and the military made democratic.

12. WE WANT THE RIGHT TO BE ECONOMICALLY INDEPENDENT OF ADULTS. We believe we are entitled to work or to unemployment benefits. Child-labor laws and extended schooling now force youth into the status of a dependent colony.

13. WE WANT THE RIGHT TO LIVE IN HARMONY WITH NATURE. We believe that to survive we must have clean air to breathe, pure food to eat, water fit to drink, products built to last, free medical care, and an end to population growth. Life exists in balance and harmony, but greed and stupidity have now sent us disastrously out of balance with our environment and earth death seems certain. Each peson must learn to live a sound ecological life, and all people together must change the economic structure of the world until the needs of the earth and its people are met.

14. WE WANT TO REHUMANIZE EXISTENCE. We believe that to do this we must recognize and deal with the invisible dictatorship of technocracy and bureaucracy. We are the crown of creation, and we announce that it is not our desitny to become robot parts of the Great Machine.

15. WE WANT TO DEVELOP COMMUNICATION AND SOLIDARITY WITH THE YOUNG PEOPLE OF THE WORLD IN OUR COMMON STRUGGLE FOR FREEDOM AND PEACE. We believe national boundaries are artificial and must inevitably be abolished. In the new world, all resources and technology must be used for the benefit of all people.

Youth will make the revolution. Youth will keep it young!
(Gross and Gross, 1977)

ONE KID'S OWN BILL OF RIGHTS
From Ann Landers' Column

Dear Ann Landers: Us kids have rights, too. Too few adults are willing to recognize this fact. I hope you will print the Bill of Rights for Kids so every parent who reads your column can see it. It's time we were treated like people.

1. I have the right to be my own judge and take the responsibility for my own actions.

2. I have the right to offer no reasons or excuses to justify my behavior.

3. I have the right to decide if I am obligated to report on other people's behavior.

4. I have the right to change my mind.

5. I have the right to make mistakes and be responsible for them.

6. I have the right to pick my own friends.

7. I have the right to say, "I don't know."

8. I have the right to be independent of the good will of others before coping with them.

9. I have the right to say, "I don't understand."

10. I have the right to say, "I don't care."

—A Reader Since Childhood in Las Vegas
In Gross and Gross, 1977.

Appendix B.

LISTING OF YOUTH-RELATED NGO's

Initials	Ref. No.*	Organization
APDSA	3778	Asian Pacific Dental Student Association
ARMSA	0091	Asian Regional Medical Student Association
BB	0195	Boy's Brigade
BSWB	0194	Boy Scouts World Bureau
BIRSH	0203	Bureau of Information and Research on Student Health
CYCHE	4294	Caribbean Youth Committee on Human Environment
CIEO	0220	Catholic International Education Office
CISV	0262	Children's International Summer Villages — International Association
CDYLA	0267	Christian Democratic Youth of Latin America
CYE	4040	Commonwealth Youth Exchange
CEESA	0402	Conference of European Engineering Students Associations
CCDYC	3881	Conservative and Christian Democratic Youth Community
CENYC	0449	Council of European National Youth Committees
EYCE	0483	Ecumenical Youth Council in Europe
EECSCUY	0514	EEC Six Capitals Union Youth
EAPPY	0578	European Association of Producers of Publications for Youth
ECYF4HC	0638	European Committee for Young Farmers and 4-H Clubs
ECYH	0681	European Community of Young Horticulturists

Listing of Youth-Related NGO's (Continued)

Initials	Ref. No.*	Organization
ECBIYO	3943	European Co-ordination Bureau for International Youth Organizations
EFLRY	3982	European Federation of Liberal and Radical Youth
EUYCD	0903	European Union of Young Christian Democrats
FAMSA	3871	Federation of African Medical Student Associations
FIYOTO	0950	Federation of International Youth Travel Organizations
GB	0998	Girl's Brigade
IACI	3456	Inter-American Children's Institute
IAPU	1090	Inter-American Parents' Union
IAAS	1249	International Association of Agricultural Students
IACYT	1181	International Association for Children's and Youth Theatres
IADS	1271	International Association of Dental Students
IAESTE	1218	International Association for the Exchange of Students for Technical Experience
IAPESGW	1326	International Association of Physical Education and Sports for Girls and Women
IASBE	1349	International Association of Students in Business and Economics
IAWMC	1374	International Association of Workers for Maladjusted Children
IAYM	1375	International Association of Youth Magistrates
IBO	1389	International Baccalaureate Office
IBBYP	1400	International Board on Books for Young People
IBTYE	1423	International Bureau for Tourism and Youth Exchanges
ICCB	1451	International Catholic Child Bureau
ICGS	1455	International Catholic Girls' Society
ICFCYP	1483	International Centre of Films for Children and Young People
ICC	1496	International Children's Center
ICCAM	1606	International Committee of Children's and Adolescents Movements
ICCS	1683	International Conference of Catholic Scouting

Listing of Youth-Related NGO's (Continued)

Initials	Ref. No.*	Organization
ICCP	1724	International Council for Children's Play
IFM—SEI	1821	International Falcon Movement—Socialist Educational International
IFCPYC	3960	International Federation of Catholic Parochial Youth Communities
IFCC	1880	International Federation of Children's Communities
IFMSA	1956	International Federation of Medical Students' Associations
IFNAES	1963	International Federation of National Associations of Engineering Students
IFOSCE	1968	International Federation of Organizations for School Correspondence and Exchange
IFTA	2021	International Federation of Teachers Associations
IFYM	2047	International Federation of Youth and Music
IFES	2048	International Fellowship of Evangelical Students
IGTYF	2082	International Good Templar Youth Federation
IHC	2101	International Help for Children
IICLRR	2123	International Institute for Children's Literature and Reading Research
IIES	2130	International Institute for Education Studies
ILF	2236	International Luge Federation
IMA	2267	International Montessori Association
IMAC	2273	International Movement of Apostolate of Children
IMCARY	2274	International Movement of Catholic Agricultural and Rural Youth
IPSF	2353	International Pharmaceutical Students' Federation
ISMUN	2597	International Student Movement for the United Nations
IUCW	2653	International Union for Child Welfare
IUIMP	2729	International Union of Individuals of Mixed Parentage
IUSY	2778	International Union of Socialist Youth
IUS	2780	International Union of Students
IUSA	2781	International Union of Students in Architecture

Listing of Youth-Related NGO's (Continued)

Initials	Ref. No.*	Organization
IUYCD	2795	International Union of Young Christian Democrats
IVSA	2802	International Veterinary Students Association
IYCSI	2825	International Young Catholic Students — International
IYCW	2826	International Young Christian Workers
IYCHE	4306	International Youth Conference on the Human Environment — Hamilton Group
IYFESC	2827	International Youth Federation for Environmental Studies and Conservation
IYHF	2828	International Youth Hostel Federation
JCSFO	2846	Joint Committee of Scandinavian Falcon Organizations
LCATUYO -EEC	2922	Liaison Committee of Agricultural Trade Union Youth Organizations of the Six Countries of the EEC
LEY	2933	Liberal European Youth
MEGTYC	2956	Middle European Good Templar Youth Council
NGO- UNICEF	2973	Non-Governmental Organizations Committee on UNICEF
NCIGTYF	3188	Nordic Council of the International Good Templar Youth Federation
NLRY	2992	Nordic Liberal and Radical Youth
NUYC	3000	Nordic Union of Young Conservatives
PAYM	3925	Pan African Youth Movement
PRIMCS	3086	Pax Romana, International Movement of Catholic Students
SJYF	3189	Scandinavian Jewish Youth Federation
SEL	3212	Scouts' Esperanto League
SOS-CV	3246	SOS-Children's Villages
SATA	3946	Student Air Travel Association
UESA	3350	Union of European Student Associations
ULAEY	3356	Union of Latin American Ecumenical Youth
WASU	4187	Western African Students Union
WAY	1054	World Assembly of Youth
WAGGS	3469	World Association of Girl Guides and Girl Scouts
WAYPF	3478	World Association of Young People's Friends
WFY	3513	World Federalist Youth

WFCY	3517	World Federation of Catholic Youth
WFDY	3519	World Federation of Democratic Youth
WFLRY	3526	World Federation of Liberal and Radical Youth
WOECE	3562	World Organization for Early Childhood Education
WSCF	3584	World Student Christian Federation
WUJS	3598	World Union of Jewish Students
WUOSY	3600	World Union of Organizations for the Safeguard of Youth
WOYE	3566	World Organization of Young Esperantists

*This is the entry number assigned to each organization in the *Yearbook of International Organizations,* and is provided for ease in looking up each organization for thoe who wish to study them further. Source: *Yearbook of International Organizations* (1974).

References

Adams, Paul, et al.
  1971   Children's Rights: Toward the Liberation of the Child. New York: Praeger.
Adelman, Irma and Cynthia Taft Morris
  1973   Economic Growth and Social Equity in Developing Countries. Stanford, California: Stanford University Press.
Alexander, J.
  1975   Foreword to Symposium: Law and the Aged. Arizona Law Review, Vol. 17:2
Alicia Patterson Fund
  1971   Various Reports from the Alicia Patterson Fund, 535 Fifth Avenue, New York, New York 10017
Allen, Edward S.
  1977   Freedom in Iowa: The Role of Iowa Civil Liberties Union. Ames: Iowa State University Press.
American Friends Service Committee
  1976   School Days, Saturdays, Sundays and Fiestas (Children Who Work in Commercial Agriculture). Philadelphia, Pennsylvania.
Andemicael, Berhanykun and Anthony J. Murdoch (eds.)
  1973   International Youth Organizations and the United Nations. New York: UNITAR.
Ariyaratne, A.T.
  1977   "A People's Movement for Self-Reliance in Sri Lank." Assignment Children, 39 (July-Sept.), pp. 78-79.
Barton, Elizabeth M., et al.
  1975   "Recent findings on adult and gerontological intelligence." American Behavioral Scientist, 19, 2
          (November/December): 224-236

Behavior Today
 1978   January 23. On access to federally financed programs by children, older people.
 1977   December 12. Story on British schoolboy's legal challenge of birching.
Bengston, Vern L. and Roberts S. Laufer (eds.)
 1974   Youth, Generations and Social Change. Special Issue of the Journal of Social Issues, 30, 3.
Bennett, William S.
 1967   "Educational change and economic development." Sociology of Education, XL (Spring): 101-114
Berg, Leila
 1971   "Moving towards self-government." pp. 9-50 in Paul Adams, et al. Children's Rights: Toward the Liberation of the Child. New York: Praeger.
Bettelheim, Bruno
 1969   The Children of the Dream: Communal Child-Rearing and American Education. New York: Macmillan.
Blackstone, Sir William
 1959   *Ehrilich's Blackstone.* Ed. J.W. Ehrlich. San Carlos, California: Nourse.
Boserup, Ester
 1970   Woman's Role in Economic Development. New York: St. Martin's Press.
Boulder Daily Camera
 1977   Boulder, Colorado, February.
Boulding, Elise
 1979a "Women and social violence." In Stephen Marks (ed.), Violence and Its Causes: Theoretical and Methodological Aspects of Recent Research on Violence. Paris: UNESCO.
 1979b "The Nurture of Adults by Children in Family Settings." In Research in the Interweave of Social Roles, Helen Lopata (ed.). Connecticut: JAI Press.
 1977a Women in the Twentieth Century World. New York: Halsted Press (A Sage Publications Book).
 1977b "The human services component of nonmarket productivity in ten Colorado households." Boulder: University of Colorado, Institute of Behavioral Science (mimeo).
 1976a The Underside of History: A View of Women Through Time. Boulder, Colorado: Westview Press.
 1976b Personhood of Children. Philadelphia: Friends General Conference.

1976 "Adolescent Culture: Reflections of Divergence." Pp. 187-220 in Nobuo Kenneth Shimahara and Adam Scrupski (eds.), Social Forces and Schooling. New York: David McKay.

1972 "The child as shaper of the future." Peace and Change: A Journal of Peace Research I, 1 (Fall).

1962 Children and Solitude. Wallingford, Pennsylvania: Pendle Hill Pamphlet.

Boulding, Elise, Shirley Nuss, Dorothy Carson and Michael Greestein
1976 Handbook of International Data on Women. New York: Halsted Press (A Sage Publications Book).

Boulding Global Data Bank
n.d. Boulder, Colorado: Institute of Behavioral Science, University of Colorado

Broadhurst, Diane D.
1975 "Project protection: a school program to detect and prevent child abuse and neglect." Children Today, IV, 3 (May/June): 22-25.

Bronfenbrenner, Urie
1970 Two Worlds of Childhood: U.S. and U.S.S.R. New York: Russell Sage Foundation.

Brownmiller, Susan
1975 Against Our Will: Men, Women and Rape. New York: Simon and Schuster.

Cain, Mead T.
1977 "The Economic Activities of Children in a Village in Bangladesh." Pp. 201-228 in Population and Development Review, Vol. 3, No. 3 (September).

Califano, Joseph A., Jr.
1970 The Student Revolution: A Global Confrontation. New York: W.W. Norton and Company.

Cavan, Ruth Shonle
1968 Deliquency and Crime: Cross-Cultural Perspectives. New York: J.B. Lippincott Company.

Childhood City Directory
1977 Distributed by the Environmental Psychology Program, the Graduate School of the City University of New York, Spring.

Children's Defense Fund
1974 Children Out of School in America. Cambridge, Massachusetts.

Clemente, Frank and Michael B. Kleiman
1976 "Fear of crime among the aged." The Gerontologist, 16, 3:207-210.

Clifford, William
  1976   Crime Control in Japan. Lexington, Massachusetts: Lexington Books.
Cobb Edith
  1977   The Ecology of Imagination in Childhood. New York: Columbia University Press.
Connor, Walter D.
  1972   Deviance in Soviet Society: Crime, Delinquency and Alcoholism. New York: Columbia University Press.
Cogwill, Donald O.
  1968   "The social life of the aging in Thailand." The Gerontologist, 8, 3:159-163.
Cry and You Cry Alone
  1978   London: Help the Aged, 32 Dover Street
Davoren, Elizabeth, Brandt F. Steele, and Jolly K.
  1975   "Working with abusive parents." Children Today, IV, 3 (May/- June): 2-9
deMause, Lloyd
  1974   "The evolution of childhood." pp. 1-74 in Lloyd deMause (ed.), The History of Childhood. New York: Psychohistory Press.
Densen-Gerber, Judianne and Jean Benward
  1975   Incest As a Causative Factor in Anti-Social Behavior: An Exploratory Study. New York: Odyssey Institute.
De Tocqueville, Alexis
  1945   Democracy in America. Translated by Philips Bradley. New York: Alfred A. Knopf, Inc.
Eckholm, Erik and Kathleen Newland
  1977   "Health and family planning factor." Worldwatch Paper Number 10 (January).
Eckholm, Erik and Frank Record
  1976   "The two faces of malnutrition." Worldwatch Paper Number 9 (December)
11 Million Teenagers
  1976   What Can Be Done About the Epidemic of Adolescent Pregnancies in the United States. New York: Alan Guttmacher Institute, Planned Parenthood Federation of America, Inc.
Elkind, David
  1970   Children and Adolescents: Interpretive Essays on Jean Piaget. New York: Oxford University Press.
Emmerson, Ronald K. (ed.)

1968　Students and Politics in Developing Nations. New York: Praeger.

Erikson, Erik

1964　Insight and Responsibility. New York: W.W. Norton and Company.

1950　Childhood and Society. New York: W.W. Norton and Company.

Fanshel, David and Eugene B. Shinn

1978　Children in Foster Care: A Longitudinal Investigation. New York: Columbia University Press.

Farson, Richard

1974　Birthrights. New York: Macmillan Publishing Company, Inc.

Fendrich, James M. and Ellis S. Krauss

1976　"Student Activism and Adult Left-Wing Politics. Politics: A Causal Model of Political Socialization for Black, White and Japanese Students of the 1960s Generation." Florida State University and Western Washington State College: unpublished paper.

Fenton, Edward

1971　Peace– It's Wonderful!: A Small Collection of Olive Branches. New York: New American Library.

Fonner, Anne (ed.)

1975　Age in Society. Special Issue of the American Behavioral Scientist, 19, 2 (November/December).

Forer, Lois G.

1973　"Rights of Children: the legal vacuum." pp. 24-36 in Albert E. Wilkerson (ed.), The Right of Children: Emergent Concepts on Law and Society. Philadelphia: Temple University Press.

Foster, Henry H., Jr.

1974　A "Bill of Rights" for Children. Springfield, Illinois: Charles C. Thomas.

Foxfire Book

1975　Edited by Eliot Wigginton. New York: Anchor/Doubleday.

1977　no. 1-3, 1975; no. 4, 1977.

Flaste, Richard

1977　"Survey finds that most children are happy at home, but fear world." New York Times, March 2. From Report by Foundation for Child Development; carried out by Zell et al. at Temple University's Institute for Survey Research.

Frisch, Rose E.

1978　"Population, Food Intake and Fertility." Science 199:4324 (January) pp. 22-30.

Frontiers
1977   Special Issue on Women's Oral History, 2, No. 2 (Summer).
Furnival, F.J. (ed.)
1931   John Russel's Boke of Nurture. Oxford England: Oxford
        University Reprint (originally published 1868).
1930   Caxton's Book of Courtesye. Oxford, England: Oxford
        University Reprint (originally published 1477-78).
Gill, David G.
1976   The Challenge of Social Equality. Cambridge, Massachusetts:
        Schenkman Publishing Co.

Gillette, Arthur
1974   "The Young Adolescent: An Untapped Resource." UNICEF
        News, 79, 1:24-27.
Gross, Beatrice and Ronald, eds.
1977   The Children's Rights Movement: Overcoming the Oppression
        of Young People. New York: Anchor Press, Doubleday.
Gutman, David
1977   "The cross-cultural perspective. Notes towards a comparative
        psychology of aging." In S. Birsen and Kieds Schaie (Eds.). Hand-
        book of the Psychology of aging. New York: Van Nostrand.
Hafen, Bruce C.
1977   "Puberty, privacy and protection: the risks of children's rights."
        American Bar Association Journal, 63 (October): 1383-1388.
Hapkiewicz, Walter G.
1975   "Research on corporal punishment effectiveness: Contributions
        and limitations." East Lansing, Michigan: Michigan State
        University (mimeo: ERIC No. EA 006 876#ED102739).
Hartley, Shirley Foster
1975   Illegitimacy. Berkeley: University of California Press.
Hastings, Elizabeth H. (ed.)
n.d.   International Youth Study Inventory. Williamstown, Massachu-
        setts: Roper Public Opinion Research Center.
Help Age International
1977   Wetford, Herts, England (January).
Hess, Robert D. and Judith V. Torney
1967   The Development of Political Attitudes in Children. Chicago:
        Aldine.
Hinners, James E.
1973   "Soviet correctional measures for juvenile delinquency." British
        Journal of Criminology, V, 13:218-227.

Holt, John
1974   Escape from Childhood. New York: E. P. Dutton.
Homan, Walter Joseph
1939   Children and Quakerism. Berkeley, California: The Gillick Press.
Huizinga, Jan
1955   Homo Ludens: A Study of the Play Element in Culture. Boston: Beacon Press.
Hurt, Maure, Jr.
1975   Child Abuse and Neglect: A Report on the Status of the Research. Washington, D.C.: United States Department of Health, Education and Welfare.
Isaacs, Susan Sutherland
1930   Intellectual Growth in Young Children. London: Routledge and Kegan Paul.
ISVS
1973   World Statistical Directory of Volunteer and Development Service Organizations. Geneva: International Secretariat for Volunteer Service.
Iyer, Subramania
1966   "Degree of protection under family allowances schemes: a statistical study of selected countries." International Labour Review, 94:477-487.
Kamerman, Sheila B.
1975   "Eight countries: cross-national perspectives on child abuse and neglect." Children Today (May/June): 34-37.
Kaplan, Jerome and Gordon J. Aldridge (eds.)
1962   Social Welfare of the Aging. New York: Columbia University Press.
Katz, Sanford N., William A. Schroeder and Lawrence R. Sidman
1973   "Emancipating our children: Coming of legal age in America." Family Law Review, 7:211-241.
Killian, Johnny H.
1978   "Constitutional Rights of Children: An Overview." Washington, D.C.: The Library of Congress, Congressional Research Service.
Kohlberg, Lawrence
1963   "The development of children's orientation toward a moral order: I. Sequence in the development of thought." Vitz Humana, 6:11-33.
Lee, Luke T.
1972   "Law, human rights and population: A strategy for action." Virginia Journal of International Law, 12, 3:309-325.

Lourie, Ira S.
1977   "Institutionalization of Child Abuse and Neglect." Keynote speech to the Conference on the Social Costs of the Maltreatment of Children at Rutgers Medical School, March 2-5.

1976   "The Phenomenon of the Abused Adolescent: A Clinical Study." Presented at the 1976 Annual Meeting of the American Academy of Child Psychiatry, October 24, Toronto, Canada.

Lowe, John
1975   The Education of Adults: A World Perspective. Paris: UNESCO.

Lowenstein, Steven
1965   Materials on Comparative Criminal Law as Based upon the Penal Codes of Ethiopia and Switzerland. Addis Ababa: Oxford University Press.

Loventhal, Marjorie Fiske, and Majda Turner, David Chiriboga and Associates
1976   Four Stages of Life. San Francisco: Jossey-Bass Publishers.

Lynch, Kevin
1977   Growing Up in Cities: Studies of the Spatial Environment of Adolescence in Cracow, Melbourne, Mexico City, Salta, Toluca and Warszawa. Paris: UNESCO and Cambridge: MIT Press.

Maas, Henry S. and Joseph A. Kuypers
1975   From Thirty to Seventy. San Francisco: Jossey-Bass Publishers.

Macdonald, John M.
1971   Rape: Offenders and Their Victims. Springfield, Illinois: Charles C. Thomas, Publisher.

Margulec, I.
1965   "The care of the aged in Israel." The Gerontologist, 5 (June): 61-66.

Maurer, Adah
1974   "Corporal punishment." American Psychologist XXIX, 8 (August): 614-626.

Mayer, Jean and Johanna Dwyer
1977   "Food for thought: grocers flunk nutrition." *Boulder Daily Camera,* July 31.

Mead, Margaret
1950   Sex and Temperament in Three Primitive Societies. New York: New American Library.

Medea, Andra and Kathleen Thompson
1974   Against Rape. New York: Farrar, Straus and Giroux.

Mendel, Gérard
   1972   "Introduction." pp. 7-8 in United Nations, Rights and Responsibilities of Youth. Number 5, Educational Studies and Documents. Paris: UNESCO.
   1971   Pour Décoloniser L'Enfant: Sociopsychanalyse de l'Autorité. Paris. Petite Bibliotheque Payot.

Milgram, Joel I. and Dorothy June Sciarral (eds.)
   1974   Childhood Revisited. New York: Macmillan.

Miller, S.M. and Pamela Roby
   1970   The Future of Inequality. New York: Basic Books, Inc.

Montagu, Ashley
   1971   Touching: The Human Significance of the Skin: New York: Columbia University Press.

Moray, Roger
   1977   "Where Fascism and Sexism Meet." London: Peace News, October 7.

Murata, Kiyoraki
   1977   "Child Suicides." The Japan Times, October 14.

Nagi, Saad Z.
   1975   "Child abuse and neglect programs: a national overview." Children today (May/June:) 13-17

National Academy of Sciences
   1973   "The relationship of nutrition to brain development and behavior." Washington, D.C.: National Academy of Sciences.

National Education Association of the U.S., Department of Elementary Principals
   1977   National Assessment of Educational Progress: 1977 Report. Washington, D.C.: NEA.

Nizalovszky, Endre
   1968   Order of the Family: Legal Analysis of Basic Concepts. Budapest: Akademiai Kiado.

Omachi, Chiyo
   1962   "Gerontology practices in Japan." The Gerontologist, 2, 1 (March): 74-76.

Ornauer, H. et al. (eds.)
   1976   Images of the World in the Year 2000: A Comparative Ten Nation Study. Atlantic Highlands, New Jersey: Humanities Press.

Paedophile Information Exchange
   1976   Press Release reported in Peace News, London, January 9.

Palmore, Erdman B. and Kenneth Manton
   1974   "Modernization and the Status of the Aged." Journal of Gerontology, Vol. 29, 2:205-210.

Papanek, Ernst
1975   Out of the Fire. New York: William Morrow.
Piaget, Jean
1932   Moral Judgment of the Child. New York: Free Press.
Picard, Georges
         "Drugs in some French dailies and periodicals." Working Paper
         for the Seminar on Youth and the Use of Drugs in Industrialized
         Countries. Paris: UNESCO.
Prasad, Devi and Tony Smythe (eds.)
1968   Conscription: A World Survey. London: War Resister's Interna-
         tional.
Prescott, James W.
1977   "Child Abuse in America: Slaughter of the Innocents." Colum-
         bus, Ohio: Reprint from Hustler Magazine.
Reilly, Mary
1974   Play as Exploratory Learning. Beverly Hills: Sage Publications.
Riley, Matilda White and Anne Foner
1968   Aging and Society. Vol I: An Inventory of Research Findings.
         New York: Russell Sage Foundtion.
Robertson, James
1976   Power, Money and Sex: Towards a New Social Balance. Lon-
         don: Marion Boyars.
Rochefort, Christine
1976   Les Enfants d'Abord. Paris: Bernard Grasset
Rockefeller Foundation
1977   Children: In Purusit of Justice. Working Papers from a
         Rockefeller Foundation Conference, February 1977. New York.
Rodham, Hillary
1973   "Children Under the Law." Harvard Educational Review, 43,
         (November): 487-514.
Rogoff, Barbara and Martha Julian Sellers, Sergio Pirrotta, Nathan Fox,
         Sheldon H. White
1976   "Age of Assignment of Roles and Responsibilities to Children: A
         Cross-Cultural Survey." In Human Development, Vol. 19, Basel:
         S. Karger AG.
Rosenberg, George S.
1970   The Worker Grows Old. San Francisco. Jossey-Bass Publishers.
Russell, Diana E. H., and Nicole Vande Ven (eds.)
1977   Proceedings of the International Tribunal on Crimes Against
         Women. Oakland, California: Mills College.

Russell, Diana E.H.
1975   The Politics of Rape: The Victim's Perspective. New York: Stein and Day.
Samuel, Raphael (ed.)
1975   Village Life and Labor. Lonseon: Routledge and Kegan Paul.
Schultz, Theodore W.
1975   "The family and the value of human time." Chicago: University of Chicago (mimeo; Human Capital Paper Number 75:3).
Schuman, Howard, Alex Inkeles and David Smith
1967   "Some psychological effects and non-effects of literacy in a new nation." Economic Development and Cultural Change, XVI (October): 1-14.
Sgroi, Suzanne M.
1975   "Sexual Molestation of children: the last frontier in child abuse." Children Today (May/June): 8-22.

Shanas, Ethel
1963   "Some observations on cross-national surveys of aging." The Gerontologist, 3, 1 (March): 7-9
Shanas, Ethel et al.
1968   Old People in Three Industrial Societies. New York: Atherton Press.
Shapiro, Michael
1977   Children of the Revels: The Boys Companies of Shakespeare's Time and Their Plays.
Social Indicators
1973   Written and compiled by the Statistical Policy Division, Office of Management and Budget, and prepared for publication by the Social and Economic Statistics Administration, U.S. Department of Commerce. Washington, D.C.
Stallibrass, Alison
1974   The Self-Respecting Child: A Study of Children's Play and Development. London: Thames and Hudson.
Stein, Herman D. (ed.)
1965   Planning for the Needs of Children in Developing Countries. New York: UNICEF.
Steinmetz, Suzanne K. and Murray A. Straus (eds.)
1974   Violence in the Family. New York: Dodd, Mead & Company.
Stone, L. Joseph, Henrietta T. Smith and Lois B. Murphy
1973   The Competent Infant: Research and Commentary. New York: Basic Books, Inc.

Struve, James
   1978   Personal communication.
Sudia, Celia
   1975   Memorandum on Santa Clara County, California—Child Sexual Abuse Treatment Program. Washington, D.C.: Department of Health, Education and Welfare.
Thomas, Bernard
   1973   La Croisade des enfants. Paris: Fayard.
Tibbitts, Clark and Wilma Donahue (eds.)
   1962   Social and Psychological Aspects of Aging. New York: Columbia University Press.
"23 Million U.S. Adults are Functionally Illiterate"
   1975   *Boulder Daily Cameras,* October 29.
United Nations
   1977a   The Aging in Slums and Uncontrolled Settlements. New York: United Nations

   1977b   "Flow of External Aid for Education at the Primary School Level and to Non-Formal Education, and UNICEF Participation." Report of the Executive Director, Executive Board 1977 Session. New York: ECOSOC. (E/ICEF/L.1358).

   1977c   "Report of the Special Meeting on the Situation of Children in Asia with Emphasis on Basic service, Manila, 17-19 May 1977." New York: ECOSOC. (E/ICEF/650/Rev. 1) (E/ICEF/ASAS/14/Rev. 1)

   1977d   Youth Institutions and Services: Present State and Development. Number 23, Educational Studies and Documents. Paris: UNESCO.

   1976a   The Aspirations of Young Migrant Workers in Western Europe. Number 21, Educational Studies and Documents. Paris: UNESCO.

   1976b   Lifelong Education: The Curriculum and Basic Learning Needs. Final report of the Regional Seminar, Chiangmai, Thailand, 7-15 June. Bangkok: UNESCO.

   1976c   United Nations Children's Fund: Report of the Executive Board (17-28 May 1976), Supplement Number 7. New York: United Nations.

   1976d   Working Paper for the Symposium of Young Workers on the Quality of Work and Work Prospects. (31 May-4 June, 1976). Paris: UNESCO. (ED-76/CONF.816/2).

   1976e   World Health Statistics Annual, Vol. 1. New York: United Nations.

1976f Yearbook of Labour Statistics. Geneva: International Labour Office.

1975a The Aging: Trends and Policies. New York: United Nations.

1975b "Current trends and changes in the status and roles of women and men and major obstacles to be overcome in the achievement of equal rights, opportunities and responsibilities." A Conference Paper for International Women's Year. New York: United Nations (E/CONF.66/3/Add.1).

1975c Service by Youth: a Survey of Eight Country Experiences. New York: United Nations.

1975d Statistical Yearbook, 1974. Paris: UNESCO.

1975e United Nations Demographic Yearbook, 1974. New York: United Nations.

1975f Yearbook of Labour Statics. Geneva: International Labour Office

1974a 1973 Demographic Yearbook. New York: United Nations.

1974b "Population and Youth." Background document for the Seminar and Groundwork to Formulate a Policy for Youth Activities in the Population Field (August 5-9, 1974). Paris: UNESCO, (ED-74/WS.32).

1974c Report of the Seminar on Youth and the Use of Drugs in Industrialized Countries. (10-15) September 1973). Paris: UNESCO (ED/MD/34).

1974d "Report on the Situation of Youth." General Conference, Eighteenth Session. Paris: UNESCO (18C/71).

1972a Final Report, International Seminar, Youth, Peace, Education, Gdansk, Poland (27 September-October, 1972). Paris: UNESCO (Ed.72/CONF. 56/3).

1972b Rights and Responsibilities of Youth. Number 6, Educational Studies and Documents. Paris: UNESCO.

1972c Youth in the Second Development Decade. Report of the Symposium on the Participation of Youth in the Second United Nations Development Decade (27 September-7 October 1971). New York: United Nations.

1971a 1970 Demographic Yearbook. New York: United Nations.

1971b Statistics of Students Abroad—1962-1968: Where They Go, Where They Come From, What They Study. Paris: UNESCO.

1971c The Status of the Unmarried Mother: Law and Practice. New York: Commission on the Status of Women (E/CN.6/540/Rev.1).

1971d Yearbook of Human Rights for 1971. New York: United Nations.

1970   Yearbook on Human Rights for 1970. New York: United Nations.

1969   1967 Report on the World Social Situation. New York. United Nations.

1966a   Children and Youth in National Development in Latin America. New York: UNICEF.

1966b   Housing for the Elderly. 2 vols. Proceedings of the Colloquim, Belgium and The Netherlands, 45-15 October, 1965. New York: United Nations.

1966c   Social Welfare and Services in Africa: Family, Child and Youth Welfare Services in Africa. New York: United Nations.

1965   The Young Adult Offender: A Review of Current Practices and Programmes in Prevention and Treatment. New York: United Nations (ST/SOA/SD/11).

1964   Provisional Report on World Population Prospects as Assessed in 1963. New York: United Nations.

United States Bureau of the Census
  1973   Series P-60, No. 91, "Characteristics of the Low-Income Population: 1972. Washington, D.C.: U.S. Government Printing Office.

Uviller, Rena K.
  1977   New York Times, April 20.

Wakin, Edward
  1975   Children Without Justice: A Report by the National Council of Jewish Women. New York: National Council of Jewish Women, Inc.

Waldock
  1965   Human Rights in Contemporary International Law and the Significance of the European Convention, 11 Int'l. & Comp. L. 073 (Supp. 1965) (the paper was delivered at the European Convention on Human Rights).

Wallerstein, Immanuel
  1976   The Modern World-System: Capitalist Agriculture and the Origins of the European World-Economy in the Sixteenth Century. New York: Academic Press, Inc.

Watts, Geoff
  1978   "Hands Off! I'm in Charge of My Life!" Help Age International, No. 6 (November/December).

Weihl, Hannah
  1970   "Jewish aged of different cultural origin in Israel." The Gerontologist, 1, 2 (Summer): 146-150.

Weiner, Florence
  1971   Peace Is You and Me: Children's Writings and Paintings on Love and Peace. New York: Avon Discus Books.

White House Conference on Children and Youth
    1971   Estes Park, Colorado, April 18-22. Report. Washington, D.C.:
            GPO
Wigmore, John Henry
    1887   Summary of the Principles of Torts, par 29-36 in "Interference
            with Social Relations." 21 American Law Review: 764-778.
Wilkerson, Albert E. (ed.)
    1973   The Rights of Children: Emergent Concepts in Law and Society.
            Philadelphia: Temple University Press.
Yearbook of International Organizations
    1974   Brussels, Belgium: Union of International Associations.
Zweig, Michael
    1967   The Idea of a World University. Edited by Harold Taylor. Car-
            bondale, Illinois: Southern Illinois University Press.

INDEX

Abortion, 28
Abuse, 68, 128-129. *See also* Child
  abuse
Accidents, 72, 78, 79, 98n
Activists, 36, 40, 45, 132
Actors, child, 17
ACWR, *see* Americans Committed to
  World Responsibility
Adolescents, 13, 17, 26-27
"Adopt-a-Grandparent" movement,
  129, 132, 133
Adulthood, 16, 17, 104. *See also*
  Minors
Africa, 10, 28, 75, 83, 124; labor force
  in, 20, 21, 116; population ages in,
  72, 111, 114
Age, 102, 107, 122, 133, 136, 138; as
  classificatory principle, 2, 3, 4; and
  employment, 58n, 115, 116, 117; as
  sorting device, 101, 102, 105, 106-
  108, 133, 136
Ageism, xiv, 6, 8, 11n, 18; definition
  of, 5
Aging, onset of, 108-109, 111
Alcohol use, 19, 79
Algeria, 21
Americans Committed to World Re-
  sponsibility (ACWR), 39
Androgyny, 105, 106, 136, 138n
Ann Arbor, Michigan, 37, 99n,
  146n-149n
Apprenticeship, 58n, 81, 82

Asia, 10, 28, 75, 124; labor force in,
  20, 21; population ages in, 72, 111,
  114
Austria, 16, 59n
Authority, 6, 30

Bangladesh, 23, 24
Basic Services (UNICEF), 92, 99n
Beating, 65, 66, 70, 71, 129
Belgium, 59n
Ben Salah, Ahmed, 94
Bettelheim, Bruno, 34, 35
Bill of Rights, A Child's, 144n-146n
Bill of Rights for Children, 144n
Bill of Rights, One Kid's Own, 149n-
  150n
Births, 28, 29, 31, 119
Blackstone, William, 95n-97n
Bloom, Alex, 16
Boston, Massachusetts, 97
Britain, 71, 128
Bulgaria, 59n

Cain, Mead T., 23
California, 66-67
Canada, 68
Capitalist countries, 61, 62, 83
Center-Periphery, 8
"Chicken porn" films, 66

West Germany, 68. *See also* Germany
Wheel of life, ii, xiv, xv, 1, 102, 138
White House Conference on Children and Youth, 38, 60n
WHO, *see* World Health Organization
Wigmore, John Henry, quoted, 62
Withdrawal phenomenon, 110, 139n
Women, 49, 57, 66, 68, 99n, 139n; Basic Services for, 92, 93; in the labor force, 93, 103, 116, 117, 118, 124; and military service, 26, 59n; mortality of, 28, 123, 124; and retirement, 106, 119, 138n; sorting processes for, 102, 103, 104, 108, 119; unmarried, 29-31, 59n
Women's International League for Peace and Freedom, 133
Work groups, 50, 51
Working youth associations, 45
World health, 72, 74
World Health Organization (WHO), 72, 133, 139n
World Statistical Directory, 51

World Student Christian Federation, 49
World Union of Jewish Students, 49
World Youth Assembly (UN), 95
World youth movements, 45

Year of the Child, *see* International Year of the Child
Yearbook of International Organizations, 42,44
Young Adult Offender, The (UN), 14
Youth, 4, 13, 39, 40, 45, 49, 50, 51, 95, 109
"Youth in the Second Development Decade" (UN), 40
Youth Institutions and Services, 41
Youth Liberation of Ann Arbor, 37, 99n, 146n-149n
Youth Seminar, International, 40
Yugoslavia, 51, 68, 94

Zambia, 139n
Zweig, Michael, 39